FOOD CULTURE IN VALMIKI RAMAYANA

Exploring the Food Heritage from Epic's Era

Anil Dharmadhikari

ISBN
Paperback 979-8-89724-980-0
Hardcase 979-8-89777-932-1

॥ ॐ श्री गणेशाय नमः ॥

|| ॐ श्री सीता रामचंद्राय नमः ||

To my beloved mother, father

For your unwavering love, endless support,
and the countless sacrifices you've made to shape my journey.
Your wisdom has guided me, your strength has inspired me,
and your belief in me has given me the courage to chase my dreams.

This book is a testament to all that you've instilled in me—patience,

resilience, and the power of imagination. I am forever grateful.

Contents

Contents

Preface

॥ रामाय रामभद्राय रामचन्द्राय वेधसे ।

॥ रघुनाथाय नाथाय सीतायाः पतये नमः ॥

I was a primary school student when Ramanand Sagar's *Ramayana* was first broadcast on national television. The serial had a profound impact on my mind, shaping their moral values and cultural understanding. The grand storytelling, coupled with devotional music and visual representation of *Ramayana*, instilled virtues like honesty, respect, and devotion.

As I grew, over a period of last 30 years with the digital revolution in India there are many versions we could find. I have also heard from various sources that the stories depicted in TV serials differ slightly from the original text. Filmmakers and showrunners often use creative liberty to adapt the epic for broader audiences. This sparked a desire in me to delve deeper into the *Ramayana* and uncover the authentic story of Bhagvan Rama.

The inspiration for this study came from the remarkable work of Dr. Nilesh Oak, a distinguished researcher known for his groundbreaking studies on the *Ramayana* and *Mahabharata*. Through meticulous analysis of planetary positions mentioned in these epics, he successfully determined the precise timelines of these historical events.

After the pandemic, I came across several of his podcast sessions, which ignited a spark in my mind. As I delved deeper, I found myself drawn to a specific aspect of the *Ramayana*—one that aligned perfectly with my academic background in Food Science. This curiosity led me to a fundamental question: why not explore the references to food in the original *Valmiki Ramayana*?

While many scholars have examined food habits in the *Ramayana*, much of the discourse has cantered around a singular debate—whether or not Rama consumed meat. Numerous studies have been conducted from both perspectives, presenting arguments for and against this idea. Additionally, there are research papers discussing the plants and animals mentioned in the epic. However, no comprehensive study has been undertaken to analyse all the food items referenced in the *Ramayana* in a holistic manner. With this understanding, I decided to purchase the *Srimad Valmiki Ramayana* (Kand 1 and 2). Since my schooling was in Marathi, I chose a version that included the original Sanskrit text along with a Marathi translation to ensure better comprehension.

Valmiki rishi composed the *Ramayana* in poetic form, adhering to specific *Sanskrit chhanda* (poetic meters). This structured style of writing, while beautiful, can occasionally lead to misinterpretations of certain words or phrases if not carefully analysed. Additionally, the epic contains many subtle and direct references that enrich our understanding of the culture, traditions, and practices of that time.

Before embarking on this research, several questions intrigued me: How did the food of the *Ramayana* era differ from the Indian cuisine of today? What insights does the text provide about the ingredients, preparation methods, and dietary practices of that time? These questions became the foundation of my study, shaping my exploration of food culture within this ancient epic. The journey was started as a self-study never thought that this will result into a book format.

If someone were to ask me, "If you had a time machine, which period would you like to go back to and experience?" my answer would be twofold: the time when Shree Rama walked the Earth and the era of Chhatrapati Shivaji Maharaj's reign in India.

Majority of references are from below main sources and few additional online resources.

1. Srimad Valmiki Ramayan (Marathi translation by Divakar Anant Ghaisas) published by Ravindra Ramachandra Pethe.

2. Valmiki *Ramayana* translated and presented by Sri Desiraju Hanumanta Rao (Bala, Aranya and Kishkindha kanda) and Sri K.M.K. Murthy (Ayodhya and Yuddha kanda) with contributions from Durga Naaga Devi and Vaasudeva Kishore (Sundara kanda) retrieved from http://www.valmikiRamayan. net/.

3. *Ramayana* Insights -I by Dr. R. Rangan.

4. Plant and animal diversity in Valmiki *Ramayana* by M Amrithalingam, C.P.R. Environmental Education Centre Chennai.

॥ रामो राजमणिः सदा विजयते ॥
Acknowledgements

Writing a book is never a solitary journey, and I am deeply grateful to the many people who have supported me along the way.

First, my heartfelt gratitude goes to my family. Your unwavering love, encouragement, and patience have been my greatest source of strength. To my son Arnav, thank you for believing in me even when I doubted myself. Your support has been my anchor through the highs and lows of this journey.

To my friends and mentors, your insightful feedback, kind words, and motivation have been invaluable. I am fortunate to have such a wonderful community of people who inspire me every day.

I sincerely thank to Dr. Nilesh Oka sir for his inspiration and knowledge sharing on various platforms. I learnt many things watching his podcasts, interviews. I extend my heartfelt gratitude—*koti koti pranam*—to the developers of this website www.valmikiRamayan. net. Desiraju Hanumanta Rao and K. M. K. Murthy. It provides the entire *Ramayana* in Devanagari, along with a detailed breakdown of each *shloka*, its English translation, and even audio recordings. This is great treasure as a starting point to anyone.

Lastly, to my readers—thank you for choosing to embark on this journey with me. Your time and attention are deeply appreciated, and I hope this book brings you something meaningful.

With gratitude,

Anil Dharmadhikari

Introduction

The epic of *Ramayana* is deeply rooted in the Indian subconscious. It is present in almost every Indian household in one form or another. It has enriched Indian culture through various mediums, including movies, TV serials, plays (Natak), Ramlila, Dashavatars, and many other forms. This epic has no boundaries of religion or nations. It is performed by not only Hindus but Buddhists and Muslims also. It has been followed on many countries like Thailand, Cambodia, Indonesia, Laos, Myanmar, Nepal, Singapore, Malaysia, and Vietnam are fulfilled by *Ramayana*. This provides the great bond of culture which unites India and the countries of Southeast Asia.

It is widely known that there are many versions of the *Ramayana* available. However, it is equally recognized that Rishi Valmiki lived during the same period as Shree Rama. As a result, the most authentic and closest account of the epic is the one written by Rishi Valmiki himself. We commonly see the *Uttar Ramayana* or *Uttar Kand* along with the main text written by Valmiki rishi. It is believed that the *Uttar Ramayana* or *Uttar Kand* is later addition and not from the original Valmiki *Ramayana*.

When studying the *Ramayana*, it is essential to understand that this epic narrates the life of Shree Rama, following his fourteen-year exile to the forest, his journeys across the forests of India in search of Sita, and the climactic war with Ravana. Rama's eventual victory over Ravana is celebrated as the triumph of good over evil. *Ramayana*, the great epic which is known for its valuable messages and ideals on various aspects like administrative, strategic, ethical, spiritual, societal and familial aspects. Beyond its captivating narrative, the *Ramayana* serves as a treasure trove of cultural references, including insights into the food habits of that era.

Rama's journey from the kingdom of Ayodhya to Chitrakoot, Dandakaranya, Kishkindha, and ultimately Sri Lanka spans a vast region of present-day India. His path remains identifiable, with enduring traditions and temples commemorating his travels. Sage Valmiki, in his epic, provides detailed descriptions of the diverse foods and culinary practices encountered at various stages of Rama's journey.

Ramanayan's wealth of knowledge, wisdom, and virtues has been passed down through generations, deeply embedded in our culture and traditions. Rama's teachings on dharma (righteousness), devotion, and leadership continue to guide society through scriptures, festivals, folklore, and rituals. From sacred texts and temple traditions to storytelling and daily practices, the legacy of Rama's ideals remains a timeless source of inspiration, shaping moral values and cultural heritage across generations.

The *Śrīmad Vālmīki Ramayana* comprises 24,000 *shlokas* (verses) in the Sanskrit language. These verses are organized into chapters called *Sargas*, each of which narrates a specific event or conveys a particular theme. The *Sargas* are further grouped into larger sections called *Kāṇḍas*, akin to the internodes of a sugarcane stem, symbolizing distinct phases of the story.

Thus, the structure of 'Srimad Valmiki *Ramayana*' is arranged into six Kandas or Books, and they are:

1. Bala Kanda (Book of Youth) [77 chapters]

2. Ayodhya Kanda (Book of Ayodhya) [119 chapters]

3. Aranya Kanda (Book of Forest) [75 chapters]

4. Kishkindha Kanda (The Empire of Holy Monkeys) [67 chapters]

5. Sundara Kanda (Book of Beauty) [68 chapters]

6. Yuddha Kanda (Book of War) [128 chapters]

Ayodhya: Kingdom, Lifestyle, Culinary and Food Traditions

Ayodhya: Kingdom, Lifestyle, Culinary and Food Traditions

Let us understand the general lifestyle in the kingdom Ayodhya first. The *Ramayana* contains numerous references to food and agriculture, offering valuable insights into the lifestyle and culture of the era. Sage Valmiki frequently mentions food items, sometimes generically and at other times with specific names, painting a vivid picture of the agricultural practices and dietary habits of the time.

One of the earliest references appears in *Bālakāṇḍa* (*Sarga* 5), where Valmiki describes the city of Ayodhya. The kingdom is portrayed as prosperous, with an abundance of cereals (*dhana dhanya*), horses, camels, cows, and donkeys.

कोसलो नाम मुदितः स्फीतो जनपदो महान् ।
निविष्टः सरयूतीरे प्रभूतधनधान्यवान् ॥ १-५-५

A great kingdom named Kosala, a joyous and a vast one well flourishing with monies and cereals, is snugly situated on the riverbanks of Sarayu. [1-5-5]

दुर्गगंभीरपरिखां दुर्गमन्यैर्दुरासदाम् ।
वाजिवारणसपूर्णां गोभिरुष्ट्रैः खरैस्तथा ॥ १-५-१३

That Ayodhya is an impassable one for trespassers, or for others invaders, owing to her impassable and profound moats, and she is abounding with horses, camels, likewise with cows and donkeys. [1-5-13]

This description sheds light on the agricultural practices and the importance of livestock in the economy. The housing in Ayodhya is dense, with every piece of land utilized and constructed upon well-leveled terrain.

गृहगाढामविच्छिद्रां समभूमौ निवेशिताम् |
शालितण्डुलसम्पूर्णामिक्षुकाण्डरसोदकाम् ||१-५-१७

The city is so prosperous that rice is abundant,
and drinking water is described as tasting
as sweet as sugarcane juice.

Valmiki rishi also mentions various Vedic rituals that involve specific food substances such as milk, yogurt (*dahi*), clarified butter (*ghee*), and honey.

Madhu (Honey) — Honey is a forest product that is mentioned in various contexts, valued for its sweetness.

ततस्तास्तं समालिंग्य सर्वा हर्षसमन्विताः |
मोदकान्प्रददुस्तस्मै भक्ष्यांश्च विविधान् शुभान् || १-१०-२०

Then all of the courtesans have embraced him and all of them with
a kind of mirthfulness in the offing, presented sweet-balls and other
varieties of best sweetmeats to him. [1-10-20]

The text even includes references to sweets, using terms like *modakān* (sweet balls) and *vividha śubhān* (various sweetmeats). These references underline the cultural significance of food in ceremonies and daily life, offering a glimpse into the culinary traditions of the era.

Agricultural practices and crops

Agricultural Practices and Crops

The *Ramayana* provides valuable insights into the agrarian society of that time, highlighting the significance of agriculture not only as an economic activity but also as a cultural and religious practice.

Phala (Fruits) — Fruits are commonly mentioned as part of the forest diet of Rama, Sita, and Lakshmana during their exile.

Mūla (Roots) — Along with fruits, roots are an essential component of the diet in the wilderness, providing nourishment during their years in the forest.

Kanda (Bulbs) — Like roots, bulbs are also foraged and consumed by the exiles as part of their diet.

Ikshu (Sugarcane) — Sugarcane or products derived from it, like juice or raw sugarcane pieces, are sometimes referenced, especially in contexts of feasts or more prosperous times.

Yava (Barley) — Barley is one of the grains mentioned in the epic, indicative of the agricultural practices of the time and used in various forms, including bread or other preparations.

Godhuma (Wheat) — Like barley, wheat is another grain that is integral to the diet and mentioned in the context of more settled areas, reflecting the agricultural base of the society.

Paddy (Rice) — Rice is a staple food mentioned in the *Ramayana*, often used in various forms, from plain steamed rice to more elaborate dishes suitable for royal feasts and religious offerings.

Tila (Sesame) — Sesame seeds are mentioned, used perhaps in cooking or as an offering. Sesame is significant in Indian culture for its use in rituals and also as a food item.

Masha (Black Gram) — This lentil is mentioned and would have been used in various dishes, providing a protein—rich component to the diet.

King Janaka's involvement in ploughing the fields when he discovered Sita is a well-known example of how even rulers actively participated in farming. This reflects the deep-rooted respect for agriculture in ancient Indian society.

अथ मे कृषतः क्षेत्रं लांगलादुत्थिता मम || १-६६-१३
क्षेत्रं शोधयता लब्धा नाम्ना सीतेति विश्रुता |

"Later, when I was ploughing the ritual field
then raised by the plough [from the furrow is a baby girl...since she is]
gained while consecrating the ritual-field, she is named as Sita,
and thus she is renowned... [1-66-13]

The mention of *Navagryayana Puja* (9 planet worship) further emphasizes the connection between agriculture and religious rituals. This ceremony, associated with offering the first harvest to ancestors (*pitrs*) and deities, aligns with similar harvest festivals still observed in India today, such as Pongal, Makar Sankranti, and Onam.

The references to various cereals like *yava* (barley), corn, wheat, and *sali* rice (winter rice) suggest a well-developed agricultural system. The multiple mentions of sugarcane cultivation further confirm the people's knowledge of advanced farming techniques.

गृहगाढामविच्छिद्रां समभूमौ निवेशिताम् |
शालितण्डुलसम्पूर्णमिक्षुकाण्डरसोदकाम् ||१-५-१७

The city is so prosperous that rice is abundant, and drinking water is described as tasting as sweet as sugarcane juice.

सुकृष्ट सीमा पशुमान् हिंसाभिर अभिवर्जितः || २-१००-४४
अदेव मातृको रम्यः श्वा पदैः परिवर्जितः |

The agricultural land not exclusively fed by rains.

कच्चित् ते दयिताः सर्वे कृषि गो रक्ष जीविनः |
वार्तायाम् संश्रितः तात लोको हि सुखम् एधते || २-१००-४७

"Are you cherishing all those who live by agriculture and cattle-rearing, O, dear borhter! The people living on agriculture and cattle-rearing indeed prosper well."

बाष्प च्छहन्नानि अरण्यानि यव गोधूमवंति च |
शोभन्ते अभ्युदिते सूर्ये नदन्द्विः क्रौन्च सारसैः || ३-१६-१६

"Covered with the dew the forests that already covered with crop fields of barley and wheat are beaming forth, together with the callings of waterfowls, at the rise of the sun. [4-16-16]

केदारस्य इव केदारः स उदकस्य निरूदकः |
उपस्नेहेन जीवामि जीवन्तीम् यत् शृणोमि ताम् || ६-५-११

Even as a paddy-field without water survives, by getting wet from a neighboring paddy-field under water, I also survive since I am hearing her as surviving.

This classification indicates that people during the *Ramayana* period recognized the challenges of monsoon-dependent agriculture and adopted irrigation techniques to ensure stable crop production. The presence of extensive river systems in the Indian subcontinent likely contributed to organized irrigation efforts, which may have included wells, canals, and reservoirs.

The *Ramayana* provides clear indications that irrigation played a crucial role in agriculture, alongside dependence on rainfall. The terms **Adevamatrika**, **Nadimatrika**, and **Devamatrika** suggest a well-understood classification of agricultural practices based on water sources:

- **Adevamatrika** – Agriculture relying on irrigation rather than rainfall.

- **Nadimatrika** – Cultivation dependent on river water.

- **Devamatrika** – Farming that depends on rainfall.

The necessity of irrigation due to the "whims of weather" also aligns with the varied climatic conditions of India, where monsoons could be unpredictable. This knowledge reflects an advanced understanding of water management and agricultural sustainability during that era.

Further references highlight the presence of gardens (*udyānas*), mango plantations, and sugarcane fields, illustrating the agricultural richness of the time. These vivid descriptions provide an indirect yet compelling picture of the landscape and lifestyle.

The *Ramayana* provides detailed insights into the agricultural practices of its time, including the tools used and the challenges faced by cultivators.

Agricultural Tools in the *Ramayana*

Farmers primarily relied on plows (langala and hala), which were drawn by bulls, indicating the use of animal power in farming. Other tools used in agricultural activities included:

- Kuddala – Hoe
- Kuthara – Axe
- Tanka – Hatchet
- Sula – Crowbar
- Datr – Sickle

These tools suggest a fairly advanced level of agricultural technology, supporting land preparation, tree-cutting, and harvesting.

Agricultural Calamities in the *Ramayana*

The six major threats to agriculture mentioned in the epic were:

- Drought (Anavrishti) – Lack of rainfall leading to crop failure.
- Floods (Ativrishti) – Excessive rainfall destroying crops.
- Locusts (Pest Attacks) – Insect swarms damaging fields.
- Rats – Rodents destroying stored grains and crops.
- Birds – Birds feeding on crops and reducing yield.
- Invasions – Raids or conflicts affecting agricultural stability.

The mention of these challenges highlights the importance of agriculture in governance, as even kings like Rama were concerned about the well-being of farmers. When Rama asked Bharata whether agricultural pursuits were free from himsa (troubles), he was likely inquiring about these six calamities, reflecting his responsibility as a ruler to ensure food security and economic stability.

This shows that ancient Indian rulers were deeply involved in agricultural welfare, implementing strategies to mitigate these risks.

Overall, the *Ramayana* portrays a society where agriculture was not only the backbone of the economy but also a key part of social and religious life.

Rama's Birth Story: The Divine Payasam

Rama's Birth Story: The Divine Payasam

Sage Valmiki narrates the well-known story of Shree Rama's birth, emphasizing the pivotal Vedic ritual, *Putrakaamesti*, performed by King Dasharatha, Rama's father. During the ceremony, a deity known as *Prajāpatya-Puruṣa* emerges from the sacrificial fire bearing a golden vessel filled with divine dessert (*payasam*). Dasharatha offers this sacred dessert to his three queens, who, upon consuming it, are blessed with sons.

दिव्यपायससंपूर्णां पात्रीं पत्नीमिव प्रियाम् ।
प्रगृह्य विपुलां दोर्भ्यां स्वयं मायामयीमिव ॥ १-१६-१५

इदं तु नृपशार्दूल पायसं देवनिर्मितम् ।
प्रजाकरं गृहाण त्वं धन्यमारोग्य वर्धनम् ॥ १-१६-१९

ततो दशरथः प्राप्य पायसं देवनिर्मितम् ।
बभूव परमप्रीतः प्राप्य वित्तमिवाधनः ॥ १-१६-२३

सोऽन्तःपुरं प्रविश्यैव कौसल्यामिदमब्रवीत् ।
पायसं प्रतिगृह्णीष्व पुत्रीयमिदमात्मनः ॥ १-१६-२६

कौसल्यायै नरपतिः पायसार्धं ददौ तदा ।
अर्धादर्धं ददौ चापि सुमित्रायै नराधिपः ॥ १-१६-२७

कैकेय्यै चावशिष्टार्धं ददौ पुत्रार्थकारणात् ।
प्रददौ चावशिष्टार्धं पायसस्यामृतोपमम् ॥ १-१६-२८

अनुचिन्त्य सुमित्रायै पुनरेव महीपतिः |
एवं तासां ददौ राजा भार्याणां पायसं पृथक् || १-१६-२९

ताश्चैवं पायसं प्राप्य नरेन्द्रस्योत्तमाः स्त्रियः |
सम्मानं मेनिरे सर्वाः प्रहर्षोदितचेतसः || १-१६-३०

ततस्तु ताः प्राश्य तदुत्तमस्त्रियो
महीपतेरुत्तमपायसं पृथक् |

हुताशनादित्यसमानतेजसोऽ-
चिरेण गर्भान् प्रतिपेदिरे तदा || १-१६-३१

The term *payasam* (a dessert made from milk, sugar or jaggery, and rice or other grains). It can be additionally flavoured with dried fruits, nuts, cardamom and saffron. This shows that the people that time were knowing the milk and milk products verywell. They knew the art and processing of Sugar and Jaggery production. The agriculture was advanced to product the crops like sugarcane, paddy nuts and other cereals.

Payasam is referenced repeatedly throughout this narrative, highlighting its cultural significance. It is described not only as a divine offering but also as a widely cherished delicacy. The mention of *payasam* recurs over 9–10 times in the text, indicating its popularity during that era. It reappears later in the *Ayodhya Kānda*, underscoring its importance in rituals and celebrations.

In Present day India, it is still known as payasam and it is made in several ways. The most popular versions are the ones made with rice and vermicelli (semiya).

The Role of Food in Ramayana's Rituals and Ceremonies

The Role of Food in
Ramayana's Rituals and Ceremonies

The second chapter- Ayodhya Kāṇḍa, the longest section of the *Ramayana*, describes life in Ayodhya before Shree Rama's exile. The narrative includes several references to generic food items such as honey, corn, and other staples of daily life. These mentions offer glimpses into the diet and agricultural practices of the citizens of Ayodhya, complementing the more elaborate descriptions found in earlier sections.

Through these accounts, the *Ramayana* provides a rich tapestry of culinary and eating practices, reflecting both the sacred and the everyday aspects of food in *Ramayana* period.

Valmiki, in his narration of the preparations for Rama's Rajya Abhishek, describes numerous rituals that involve the use of various food items, including milk, curd, honey, rice, corn, and other offerings.

सुवर्णादीनि रत्नानि बलीन् सर्वौषधीरपि || २-३-८

शुक्लमाल्यांश्च लाजांश्च पृथक्च मधुसर्पिषी |

अहतानि च वासांसि रथं सर्वायुधान्यपि || २-३-९

Gather the following in the sacred fire house of the king at dawn: gold and the like, diamonds, things needed to perform worship, various herbs, white floral garlands, corn, honey and clarified butter in separate vessels.

प्रशस्तमन्नं गुणवद्बद्धिक्षीरोपसेचनम् |
द्विजानां शतसाहस्रे यत्प्रकाममलं भवेत् || २-३-१४

*"Let fine rice (prashthaannam)of good quality with milk (khira)
and curd (dadhi), fully sufficient for one hundred thousand
Brahmans be arranged."*

सत्कृत्य द्विजमुख्यानां श्वः प्रभाते प्रदीयताम् |
घृतं दधि च लाजाश्च दक्षिणाश्चापि पुष्कलाः || २-३-१५

*"Let that rice be given with due respect to important Brahmans
tomorrow at dawn; along with clarified butter (dhrutam), curd
(dhadhi), corn (lajaksh), and lot of gifts."*

तस्य नन्दन्ति मित्राणि लब्ध्वाऽमृतमिवाऽमराः || २-३-४५
तस्मात्त्वमपि चात्मानं नियम्यैवं समाचर |

*Like the celestials becoming happy after obtaining the nectar
(amrut), friends of a king (ruler of earth) are delighted when he fills
the granaries and armories to the brim, making the common people
delightful and happy. Hence, you too act like this."*

सर्वबीजानि गन्धाश्च रत्नानि विविधानि च || २-१४-३५
क्षौद्रम् दधि घृतं लाजा दर्भाः सुमनसः पयः |

*All seeds and fragrances and gems of various kinds || 2-14-35. Honey,
yogurt, butter, laja, darbas, flowers and milk.*

दध्यक्षतहविर्लाजैर्धूपैरगुरुचंदनैः || २-१७-६
नानामाल्योपगंधैश्च सदाभ्यर्चितचत्वरम् |

*All the road junctions there were regularly worshipped with yoghurt,
unbroken rice, clarified butter, fried grain, incense, aloe and sandal
and all types of garlands and perfumes.*

When Rama meets Bharat at Chitrakuta, he got to know about the death of his father king Dasharatha. Rama performed the rituals to pay homage to his dead father. He offered the balls of food (Pind daan). For making the balls he used food (Rice) and the pulp of Ingudi plum. This shows this shows that the few rituals are still the same in present day India. They are testes with the time and various challenges ans still in practice.

तततो मन्दाकिनीतीरात्प्रत्युत्तीर्य स राघवः |
पितुश्चकार तेजस्वी निवापं ब्रातृभिः सह || २-१०३-२८

Thereafter, the glorious Rama, resending the bank of Mandakini River along with his brothers, offered balls of food (Pind)to his father.

ऐङ्दम् बदरीमिश्रम् पिण्याकम् दर्भसंस्तरे |
न्यस्य रामस्स दुःखार्तो रुदन्वचनमब्रवीत् || २-१०३-२९

Rama placed the pulp of the Ingudi tree (Edgudam-Hingan bet) mixed with the pulp of plums on a mat of Kusa grass and overcome with sadness, weeping, spoke the following words: (Badari- Bor pulp)

Articles kept for worship at Kausalya's Palace

As Rama entered his mother Kausalya's palace, his gaze fell upon the sacred articles meticulously arranged for the upcoming ceremony.

देवकार्यनिमित्तम् च तत्रापश्यत् समुद्यतम् |
दध्यक्षतम् घृतम् चैव मोदकान् हविषस्तदा || २-२०-१७

लाजान् माल्यानि शुक्लानि पायसम् कृसरम् तथा |
समिधः पूर्णकुम्भांश्छ ददर्श रघुनंदनः || २-२०-१८

There, Rama saw the articles of worship kept ready for the purpose of the sacred ceremony like curd, unbroken rice, clarified butter, sweet meats, things fit for oblation, fried grain, garlands made of white flowers, rice boiled in milk, mixture of rice and peas with a few spices, sacrificial sticks, vessels full of water etc.

It is evident that the commonly used food articles used in rituals are unbroken rice, Ghee, curd, milk, honey, and corn.

Dairy products such as milk, curd, and ghee were integral to various rituals, highlighting the prominence of a cow-based economy in ancient times. Historical accounts frequently reference kings donating cows to Brahmanas and others, emphasizing the cultural and economic significance of such practices. These donations often facilitated self-sufficiency among recipients.

Cows indirectly contributed to agriculture by providing bulls for farming activities, bullock carts for transportation, and organic manure to enrich the soil. Agriculture flourished during this period, as evidenced by references to "dhan dhanya" (wealth of grains) such as rice and corn. The people of the time demonstrated expertise in processing grains, including frying, and puffing cereals.

Valmiki's works frequently mention sugarcane, indicating that the cultivation of sugarcane and the production of sugar candy and various sweets were well-established. The word 'ikshu' means sugarcane, there was a great king ancestor of Rama named- ikshukaku on his name the dynasty is known as Ikshukaku dynasty. There are also references to oilseeds, such as svetha sarshhapaan (white mustard seeds, 2-25-28). The presence of mango orchards suggests an advanced understanding of horticulture and mango cultivation.

The art of honey collection and wine production from honey was also well-known. Additionally, people were skilled in preparing diverse dishes, drinks, and syrups, as described in ancient texts (2-50-39).

As the description of exile comes many times in this book, the words such as Similar generic foods are mentioned several times. Terms such as *'Dhan-Dhanya,' 'phal-mule' 'mishtaani' peyam* (drinks), 'lehyam' syrups; mukhyaani describing the food during exile.

Ghee (clarified butter) the pure fat

Ghee, a type of clarified butter, holds a significant place in Indian culture as both a traditional medicine and a key component of Hindu religious rituals. It is considered one of the purest offerings and is commonly used in sacred ceremonies, along with other dairy products like milk and curd.

In Vedic yajñas and homas (fire rituals), ghee is an essential requirement, serving as an oblation offered to various deities through the medium of Agni (fire). Its use is deeply rooted in the spiritual and symbolic aspects of these ceremonies, signifying purity, and sustenance.

The Sanskrit term *ghṛta* refers to ghee and appears extensively in Valmiki *Ramayana*. Notably, it is mentioned multiple times in the *Ayodhya Kanda*, which describes numerous rituals performed during the preparations for Shree Rama's coronation. These references underscore the integral role of ghee in both spiritual practices and royal ceremonies during *Ramayana* times.

In the below shloka, kuluguru Vashistha give instructions referring to Ghee, curd, corn and other gifts.

सत्कृत्य द्विजमुख्यानां श्वः प्रभाते प्रदीयताम् |
घृतं दधि च लाजाश्च दक्षिणाश्चापि पुष्कलाः || २-३-१५

"Let that rice be given with due respect to important Brahmans tomorrow at dawn; along with clarified butter, curd, corn, and lot of gifts."

सर्वबीजानि गन्धाश्च रत्नानि विविधानि च || २-१४-३५
क्षौद्रम् दधि घृतं लाजा दर्भाः सुमनसः पयः |

All seeds and fragrances and gems of various kinds. Honey, yogurt, butter, laja, darbas, flowers and milk.

दध्यक्षतहविर्लाजैर्धूपैरगुरुचंदनैः || २-१७-६
नानामाल्योपगंधैश्च सदाभ्यर्चितचत्वरम् |

All the road junctions there were regularly worshipped with yoghurt, unbroken rice, clarified butter, fried grain, incense, aloe and sandal and all types of garlands and perfumes.

घृतम् श्वेतानि माल्यानि समिधः श्वेतसर्षपान् || २-२५-२८
उपसम्पादयामास कौसल्या पमाङ्गना |

Kausalya, the excellent woman procured clarified butter, white garlands, ceremonial sticks, and white mustard seeds.

मधुदध्यक्षतघृतैः स्वस्तिवाच्य द्विजाम् स्ततः || २-२५-३०
वाचयामास रामस्य वने स्वस्त्ययनक्रियाः |

She then got brahmanas to pronounce blessings with honey, curd, unbroken grains of rice and clarified butter by the repetition of certain hymns and to utter prayers for the well - being of Rama in the forest.

Notably, we can see that Ghee, curd, milk, honey, rice, corn these are the commonly used in yajñas and homas (fire rituals).

Ghee is also seen its importance in funeral rituals also. Its reference can be found in the funeral description of Vanar King Bali. It was mentioned that let Angada bring different things along with Ghee and oils to perform the funeral.

अंगदः तु आनयेत् माल्यम् वस्त्राणि विविधानि च |
घृतम् तैलम् अथो गन्धान् यत् च अत्र समनंतरम् || ४-२५-१६

Let Angada bring wreaths, different cloths,
ghee, oils, as well perfumes and other items that are
consequently useful in funeral. [4-25-16]

Story of Meru desert and Rama's boon associated with Ghee

In the *Yuddha Kand*, when Rama and Laxman reached the seashore along with the *Vanara Sena* (monkey army), they faced a significant challenge: how to cross the vast ocean to reach Lanka. Rama prayed to the sea god for several days, humbly requesting a solution. However, when there was no response from the sea, Rama grew angry and decided to use the *Brahmastra*—a celestial missile presided over by Brahma—to dry up the ocean and create a path to Lanka.

Just as Rama was about to release the powerful missile, the sea god appeared before him in person, with joined palms, pleading for peace. He advised Rama to construct a bridge across the ocean, with the help of Nala, an architect among the *Vanaras*. He assured Rama that this bridge would enable his army to cross the ocean and continue their quest to rescue Sita.

Diver this arrow Towards my northern side, there is a holy place. It is well known as Drumatulya, in the same way as you are well known to this world.

Pleased with the sea god's wisdom, Rama granted a boon to the desert region of Meru (modern-day Maru-Malwar, located in Rajasthan, India). He blessed the area to be a congenial place for cattle rearing, free from most diseases, producing abundant clarified butter (*ghee*), milk, and sweet-smelling herbs. He also blessed it to yield delicious fruits and roots.

The effects of Rama's boon are evident even today. Rajasthan, particularly the Maru-Malwar region, is renowned for its sweets and their generous use of *ghee* in preparations, a hallmark of its culinary tradition. The region remains agriculturally significant and reflects the blessings conferred upon it in the *Ramayana*.

पशव्यश्चाल्परोगश्च फलमूलरसायुतः |

बहुस्नेहो बहुक्षीरः सुगन्धिर्विविधौषधिः || ६-२२-४१

एवमेतैर्गुणैर्युक्तो बहिभिः सम्युतो मरुः |

रामस्य वरदानाच्च शिवः पन्था बभूव ह || ६-२२-४२

Due to granting of a boon by Rama, that desert of Maru became the most congenial place for cattle rearing, a place with a little of disease, producing tasty fruits and roots, with a lot of clarified butter, a lot of milk and various kinds of sweet- smelling herbs. Thus it became an auspicious and suitable move, bestowing these merits.

In Ayodhya Kand, there is description of oils used for massage as below

उत्साद्य स्नापयन्ति स्म नदी तीरेषु वल्गुषु |

अप्य् एकम् पुरुषम् प्रमदाः सत्प च अष्ट च || २-९१-५४

Seven or eight young women bathed every single man on the beautiful river-banks, after massaging their body with oil.

In Yuddha kand, there is a description of and axe which was polished with oils to prevent it from rusting. This indicates that, they were knowing the chemistry of iron rusting, and they also knew that oils can be used to prevent rusting.

Meat in rituals– There are multiple references of usage of meat in rituals. While crossing the river Ganga with the help of Guha the Nishadraj (The king of Nishadh) Sita prayed to the river Ganga and she mentioned the offerings, including meat, in lieu of Rama's safe return from his exile. Interestingly here the meat and wines both are mentioned.

सुराघटसहस्रेण मांसभूतोदनेन च |
यक्ष्ये त्वाम् प्रयता देवि पुरीम् पुनरुपागता || २-५२-८९

"Oh, goddess! After reaching back the city of Ayodhya, I shall worship you with thousand pots of spirituous liquor and jellied meat with cooked rice well prepared for the solemn rite."

One such prominent reference is at the time of their exile in the forest. Laxman builds the Hut (*Parna Kuti*) for their stay and Rama, Laxman does the in house warming ceremony where they use the meat of deer. Rama spoke the following words to Lakshmana who listened to his command and who was closely attentive to him.

ऐणेयम् मांसम् आहृत्य शालाम् यक्ष्यामहे वयम् |
कर्त्यम् वास्तुशमनम् सौमित्रे चिरजीविभिः || २-५६-२२

"Oh, Lakshmana! Bring the meat of an antelope. We shall perform a purifactory ceremony while entering the house. Which is to be done by those who wish to live long."

मृगम् हत्वाऽऽनय क्षिप्रम् लक्ष्मणेह शुभेक्षण
कर्तव्यः शास्त्रदृष्टो हि विधिर्धर्ममनुस्मर || २-५६-२३

"Oh, large-eyed Lakshmana! Killing the antelope quickly, bring it here. The prescribed rite according to scriptural point of view indeed is to be performed. Keep in mind the sacred obligation."

Rama, Laxman, and Sita satisfied the sirits by crowns of flowers obtained in the forest, by fruits roots and cooked meat, by water, by prayers as uttered in the sacred texts (Vedas).

वन्यैर्माल्यैः फलैर्मूलैः पक्कैर्मांसैर्यथाविधि |
अद्भर्जपैश्च वेदोक्तै र्धर्भैश्च ससमित्कुशैः || २-५६-३४
तौ तर्पयित्वा भूतानि राघवौ सह सीतया |
तदा विविशतुः शालाम् सुशुभाम् शुभलक्षणौ || २-५६-३५

Rama and Lakshmana along with Sita, having auspicious characteristics, satisfied the sirits by crowns of flowers obtained in the forest, by fruits roots and cooked meat, by water, by prayers as uttered in the sacred texts (Vedas), by sacred grass, by fuel and Kusa grass and then entered the auspicious leaf-hut.

All of them (Sita, Rama, and Lakshmana) together, entered that hut, thatched with leaves of trees, looking beautiful, well-constructed at a suitable site, and protected from winds, as if entering an assembly-hall called Sudharma (in heaven) by a group of celestials.

Valmiki provides a detailed account of Jatayu's funeral. As a close friend of King Dasharatha, Jatayu was honoured by Rama, who regarded it as his duty to perform the final rites, just as a son would for his father. The rituals described by Valmiki indicate that Rama and Laxman hunted a robust, large-bodied Rohi or Kesari animal. They then spread sacred grass on the ground as an offering to honour the departed soul of the noble bird.

एवम् उक्त्वा चिताम् दीप्ताम् आरोप्य पतगेश्वरम् |
ददाह रामो धर्मात्मा स्व बन्धुम् इव दुःखितः || ३-६८-३१

On saying that way, that ethical-souled Rama mounted that
Shree of birds onto the pyre and he sorrowfully incinerated
that eagle in a flaring fire of pyre, as he would
do in respect of his own deceased relative.

रामो अथ सह सौमित्रिः वनम् यात्वा स वीर्यवान् |
स्थूलान् हत्वा महा रोहीन् अनु तस्तार तम् द्विजम् || ३-६८-३२

Then that resolute Rama on going into forest along with
Soumitri hunted a robust-bodied, big Rohi animal, or, Kesari animal,
and then he spread sacred grass on ground to place that offering to
the deceased soul of that bird.

रोहि मांसानि च उद्धृत्य पेशी कृत्वा महायशाः |
शकुनाय ददौ रामो रम्ये हरित शाद्वले || ३-६८-३३

On drawing up the flesh of that Rohi animal and
lumping it to gobbets, that highly observant Rama placed
those gobbets on pleasant greenish pasturelands as obsequial
offerings in respect of that bird Jataayu.

यत् तत् प्रेतस्य मर्त्यस्य कथयन्ति द्विजातयः |
तत् स्वर्ग गमनम् पित्र्यम् क्षिप्रम् रामो जजाप ह || ३-६८-३४

Rama immediately chanted Vedic hymns that are employed in such
funerals of one's own paternal people, as Brahmans say that those
hymns are employable in such rites as they lead the soul of the
departed to heaven.

Vasistha Rishi and Shabala: The Divine Feast

Vasistha Rishi and Shabala: The Divine Feast

This story originates in the *Bal Kanda* and recounts the redemption of Ahalya from her curse when Shree Rama enters her hermitage. Ahalya is reunited with her husband, Sage Gautama, and their son, Sage Shatananda. Shatananda relates the legend of Sage Vishvamitra to Rama. In this narrative, Shatananda expresses admiration for Rama's adherence to righteousness, a quality also exhibited by Vishvamitra through his transformation from a once-powerful king to a revered sage.

Shatananda deems it significant to narrate Vishvamitra's biography to Rama, emphasizing the lessons to be learned from the king's journey. The story illustrates the consequences of excessive pride and ambition, traits that Vishvamitra initially embodied, which are deemed unbecoming for rulers.

The tale also delves into the interaction between Sage Vashishta and King Vishvamitra during the latter's reign. Vashishta, known for his wisdom and hospitality, welcomes Vishvamitra and his vast army to his hermitage. Although King Vishvamitra hesitates to burden a hermit with such a significant responsibility, Vashishta insists on hosting the king and his retinue. To fulfil this obligation, Vashishta summons Shabala, the Divine Sacred Cow, also known as Kamadhenu. Shabala produces an abundance of sumptuous food for a royal feast and provisions for the army, demonstrating the sage's extraordinary powers and his generous spirit.

The feast included an array of delicacies: dishes made from sugarcane and honey, alongside an assortment of flakes such as cornflakes and rice flakes. Fine arracks and liquors were also served, complemented by a variety of savoury side dishes and desserts crafted from rice. There were delectable dumplings made from cooked pulses, along with cascades of curds and a rich assortment of milk products, including butter, ghee, and cheese. Additionally, refreshing soft drinks sweetened with sugar candy completed the sumptuous banquet.

Below are the actual references in the Valmiki Ramayan along with the translations.

इक्षून्मधूंस्तथा लाजान् मैरेयांश्च वरासवान् |
पानानि च महार्हाणि भक्ष्यांश्चोच्चावचांस्तथा || १-५३-२

Shabala bestowed dishes of sugar cane and honey, and flakes of all sorts, like cornflakes, rice-flakes, also best arracks, and liquors in best wineglasses, further, the drinks and foodstuffs that are very diverse and verily apposite to royalties and army-men.

At Rishi Vashishat's request, Shabala produces an extraordinary array of food and drink, including sugarcane (ikSuun)and honey (madhuun), rice flakes (lājān), arracks, and liquors served in fine wineglasses.

उष्णाढ्यस्यौदनस्यापि राशयः पर्वतोपमाः |
मृष्टान्नानि च सूपाश्च दधिकुल्यास्तथैव च || १-५३-३
नानास्वादुरसानां च खाण्डवानां [षाडवानां] तथैव च |
भाजनानि [भोजनानि] सुपूर्णानि गौडानि च सहस्रशः || १-५३-४

There emerged mountainous stacks of steamy foodstuffs, palatable side-dishes, and desserts of rice etc., also the dumplings of cooked pulses, like that the cascades of curds and the other milk products like butter, ghee, cheese etc. Thousands of silver dishes and hollowware fully replete with daintily soft drinks, like that full of sugar-candy preparations, and with preparations that comprise all the six tastes have come up together with delectable foodstuffs made out of treacly dumplings of cane sugar. [1-53-3, 4]

Mountains of steamy dishes, palatable side-dishes, rice-based desserts (mistaannaani), dumplings made of cooked pulses (*gaudani*), and cascades of milk products such as curds (*dadhikulyaah*), butter, ghee, and cheese are mentioned. The feast also includes silver dishes brimming with sugar-candy (*khaaNDavanaam*) preparations, and delicacies embodying the six tastes (*saḍrasa*) (naanaasvaadurasaanaam) varied daintily soft-drinks, The abundance and variety emphasize not only the richness of Vedic hospitality but also the sophistication of culinary practices during that time.

Rishi Bharadwaja's Grand Feast for Bharata and His Army

Rishi Bharadwaja's Grand Feast
for Bharata and His Army

An interesting and significant episode unfolds in the *Ramayana*, centring around Rishi Bharadwaja and Bharata. This story takes place as Bharata, deeply desiring to see Rama, Sita, and Lakshmana during their exile, embarks on a journey to persuade them to return to Ayodhya.

On his way, Bharata meets Guha, a devoted ally of Rama, who guides him to the hermitage of Rishi Bharadwaja. Accompanied by the royal preceptor, Guru Vasishta, Bharata proceeds to meet the revered sage. Upon their arrival, Rishi Bharadwaja warmly welcomes them with great hospitality. After exchanging pleasantries, the sage poses a pointed question to Bharata, inquiring whether his visit to the forest is with any ill intent toward Rama and Lakshmana. Bharata, with sincerity, assures Bharadwaja that his sole purpose is to request Rama to return to Ayodhya and assume his rightful place as king.

When Bharata seeks information on Rama's whereabouts, Rishi Bharadwaja informs him that Rama, along with Sita and Lakshmana, is residing on Chitrakuta Mountain. Accepting the sage's invitation, Bharata decides to spend the night at the hermitage and continue his journey to Chitrakuta the following morning.

In preparation for this stay, Rishi Bharadwaja makes a remarkable request. He instructs Bharata to bring his entire entourage, including his army, to the hermitage. The sage then invokes the divine architect, Visvakarma, requesting him to prepare an extraordinary display of hospitality for Bharata and his companions.

Valmiki, the great poet–sage and chronicler of the *Ramayana*, provides a vivid and detailed description of the evening. Visvakarma arranges a sumptuous feast, presenting a dazzling array of delicacies and beverages. Rishi Bharadwaja further calls upon the three divine deities—Yama, Varuna, and Kubera—along with Indra, the king of gods, to enhance the arrangements for this grand reception.

This episode exemplifies the unparalleled generosity and spiritual grandeur of Rishi Bharadwaja, as well as the divine interventions that embellish the epic journey of Bharata in his quest to reunite with his beloved brother, Rama.

Valmiki rishi narrates this quite in detail providing the details of variety of food items and various dinks.

अन्याः स्रवन्तु मैरेयम् सुराम् अन्याः सुनिष्ठिताम् |
अपराः च उदकम् शीतम् इक्षु काण्ड रस उपमम् || २-९१-१५

"Let some rivers flow with Maireya (a kind of wine made from date palms etc) some others flow with highly refined spirituous liquor and some others flow with cool water with a taste of sugarcane."

इह मे भगवान् सोमो विधत्ताम् अन्नम् उत्तमम् |
भक्ष्यम् भोज्यम् च चोष्यम् च लेह्यम् च विविधम् बहु || २-९१-२०

"Many the blessed moon-god furnish me at this place, excellent food of every variety, confections, sweets, sauces and syrups."

विचित्राणि च माल्यानि पादप प्रच्युतानि च |
सुरा आदीनि च पेयानि मांसानि विविधानि च || २-९१-२१

"May the blessed moon-god furnish me many-coloured flowers which have just fallen from the flower-plants or trees, the drinks like wine and others as also various kinds of meat."

तस्मिन् बिल्वाः कपित्थाः च पनसा बीज पूरकाः |
आमलक्यो बभूवुः च चूताः च फल भूषणाः || २-९१-३०

At that place, Bilva, Kapittha, Panasa, Citron Amalaki and Mango Trees laden with fruit appeared.

ततः तत्र मुहूर्तेन नद्यः पायस कर्दमाः |
उपातिष्ठन्त भरतम् भरद्वाजस्य शासनत् || २-९१-४१

Then, on an instant, by the orders of Bharadwaja, streams having milk thickened with rice in the place of mud, flowed towards Bharata.

शिंशपा आमलकी जम्बूर् याः च अन्याः कानने लताः |
मालती मल्लिका जातिर्याश्चान्याः कानने लताः || २-९१-५१
प्रमदा विग्रहम् कृत्वा भरद्वाज आश्रमे अवसन् |

Shimshapas (Ashoka trees), Amalakis (Emblic myrobalan), Jambus (rose-apple trees), Malati, Mallika Jati and other creepers in the forest had been changed into dancing girls in the hermitage of Bharadwaja and they spoke as follows:

सुराम् सुरापाः पिबत पायसम् च बुभुक्षिताः || २-९१-५२
मांसनि च सुमेध्यानि भक्ष्यन्ताम् यावद् इग्च्छथ || २-९१-५३

O, winebibbers! Drink the wine, however much you desire! O troops stricken with hunger! Come and eat the Paayasam and the meats which are very much fresh.

इक्षूमः च मधु जालामः च भोजयन्ति स्म वाहनान् |
इक्ष्वाकु वर योधानाम् चोदयन्तो महा बलाः || २-९१-५७

The animals, belonging to the exceedingly strong and illustrious warriors, the descendent of Ikshvaku, were fed with pieces of sugarcane and roasted grain soaked in honey, duly cajoling them to eat.

आजैः च अपि च वाराहैर् निष्टान वर संचयैः |
फल निर्यूह संसिद्धैर् सूपैर् गन्ध रस अन्वितैः || २-९१-६८
पुष्प ध्वजवतीः पूर्णाः शुक्लस्य अन्नस्य च अभितः |
ददृशुर् विस्मिताः तत्र नरा लौहीः सहस्रशः || २-९१-६९

Dishes of goat and boar with delicious sauces were there and condiments that were spicy, fragrant, and succulent, cooked in fruit juices; vessels of rare metals filled with rice, decorated with flowers, were offered in thousands to those soldiers there. The soldiers saw them with wonder on all sides.

बभूवुर् वन पार्श्वेषु कूपाः पायस कर्दमाः |
ताः च कामदुघा गावो द्रुमाः च आसन् मधुश्च्युतः || २-९१-७०

The wells in various sides of the forest (surrounding Bharadwaja's hermitage) have their mud transformed into Paayasam. The cows in the region were transformed into cows of plenty and the trees dripped honey.

वाप्यो मैरेय पूर्णाः च मृष्ट मांस चयैर् वृताः |
प्रतप्त पिठरैः च अपि मार्ग मायूर कौक्कुटैः || २-९१-७१

Some ponds there were endowed with full of wine and some were filled with assortment of various dressed meats pertaining to deer, peacocks, and wild cocks; cooked in hot pans.

पात्रीणाम् च सहस्राणि शात कुम्भमयानि च |
स्थाल्यः कुम्भ्यः करम्भ्यः च दधि पूर्णाः सुसंस्कृताः || २-९१-७२
यौवनस्थस्य गौरस्य कपित्थस्य सुगन्धिनः |

There were thousands of portable furnaces, lacs of culinary utensils ten crores of golden vessels, well-cleaned bowls filled with curds, small water-jars, and wide-mouthed dishes.

हृदाः पूर्णा रसालस्य दध्नः श्वेतस्य च अपरे |

बभूवुः पायसस्य अन्ते शर्कराया: च संचयाः || २-९१-७३

कल्कामः चूर्ण कषायामः च स्नानानि विविधानि च |

दद्दशुर् भाजनस्थानि तीर्थेषु सरिताम् नराः || २-९१-७४

*Lakes full of fresh curds, shining fragrant and in the colour
of a wood-apple, curds mixed with sugar and spices (Srikhand),
some other lakes filled with white curds, some others filled with
Paayasam as well as sugar and some other lakes with a mixture of
barley and sugar were formed.*

Valmiki Rishi describes the lavish hospitality arranged by Rishi Bharadwaja for Bharata and his army. It includes an array of wines and liquors, such as those made from date palm and other refined spirits. A variety of fruits, including bilva, kapittha, mango, rose apple, and citron, were offered alongside dressed meats from deer, peacocks, wild cocks, goat, and boar, all prepared with delicious sauces and condiments. The feast also featured an assortment of sweets, confections, syrups, and delicacies like srikhand, payasam, and barley-sugar mixtures. Additionally, lakes of curds, sugar, and fruit juices were created, and animals such as horses, elephants, and bulls were fed roasted grain soaked in honey and pieces of sugarcane, completing the grand display of generosity and abundance.

These two feasts—one hosted by Rishi Vashistha and the other by Rishi Bharadwaja—are among my favorite chapters in the entire epic, as they provide abundant direct references to food. These accounts highlight the remarkable diversity of culinary offerings available during that era, many of which bear striking similarities to present-day foods. Furthermore, they serve as evidence of the advanced agricultural practices of the time, demonstrating the ability to cultivate and sustain a wide variety of food resources.

The Devotion of Sabari: A Tale of Faith and Love

The Devotion of Sabari:
A Tale of Faith and Love

The story of Shree Rama visiting Shabri, where she offers him partially eaten berries, is not explicitly mentioned in the Valmiki *Ramayana*. While the text does recount Shabri offering fruits to Rama, it does not describe her tasting them beforehand—a detail that features prominently in later retellings of the *Ramayana*, particularly in the Padma Purana and Tulsidas' Ramacharitmanas.

This addition in subsequent versions is often interpreted as a profound expression of devotion. It symbolizes Rama's acceptance of pure, heartfelt devotion irrespective of social status, as Shabri is frequently depicted as a humble tribal woman.

The story emphasizes the inclusivity of Rama's divine grace and has become a celebrated example of bhakti (devotion) in Indian tradition. The story of Shabri tasting the berries is believed to have been embellished in later retellings of the *Ramayana* to emphasize the egalitarian nature of Rama's character and his acceptance of devotion from all levels of society.

एवम् उक्ता महाभागैः तदा अहम् पुरुषर्षभ |
मया तु विविधम् वन्यम् संचितम् पुरुषर्षभ || ३-७४-१७
तव अर्थे पुरुषव्याघ्र पम्पायाः तीर संभवम् |

"Oh, best one among men Rama,
thus I was told by those highly providential sages,
oh, best one among men, oh, manly tiger,
and I have gleaned various forest fruits and eatables
that occur on the moorlands of Pampa Lake for your sake..."
So said Shabari to Rama.

The Valmiki *Ramayana* recounts the story of Shabari collecting fruits for Shree Rama and Laxman and offering them with great devotion. However, it does not mention the widely popular detail that she tasted the fruits first to ensure they were sweet before offering them to Shree Rama.

This particular element of the story first appears in the Padma Purana, where Shabari is described as tasting the fruits herself to check for bitterness before presenting them to Rama, who accepted them with pleasure.

In the Valmiki *Ramayana*, it is mentioned that after feeding Shree Rama and Laxman with fruits, Shabari showed them her ashrama. Following this, Shree Rama blessed her, and her pure soul ascended to heaven.

The depiction of her unwavering devotion has since become an enduring symbol of selfless love and faith in Indian spiritual traditions.

The Vanar Sena's Diet: Fuelling the Mighty Warriors of Rama

The Vanar Sena's Diet: Fuelling the Mighty Warriors of Rama

Food is a basic requirement for any living being. The Vanar Sena's diet in the *Ramayana* aligns with their nature as forest dwellers, relying on fruits, roots, and honey for sustenance. In Kishkindha Kand, Valmiki describes that Sugreev asks Vanar chiefs go round the earth to fetch all the Vanar champions on earth to the presence of Sugreeva. They all go to different mountain, rivers, oceans, and forests and motivate all Vanars to reach Sugreeva at once. Further, having gone to Himalayas they found divine fruits, tubers, and medicinal herbs there, which they fetch as royal gifts to Sugreeva.

फल मूलेन जीवन्तो हिमवन्तम् उपाश्रिताः |
तेषाम् कोटि सहस्राणाम् सहस्रम् समवर्तत || ४-३७-२३

Those that are sheltered on Himalayas subsisting on fruits and tubers have arrived in a thousand of thousand crores, say a trillion. [4-37-23]

क्षीर उद वेला निलयाः तमाल वन वासिनः |
नारि केल अशनाः चैव तेषाम् संख्या न विद्यते || ४-३७-२५

The count of those vanara-s who are basically domiciled at the coasts of milky ocean, the residents of Tamala woodlands, and those who feed on coconuts dwelling in coconut groves, and who have presently come from those places is uncountable.

Dr. Murthi says – 'The milky ocean referred here is not to be construed as that of Vishnu. The word used for coconut here is naari kela whereas the real Sanskrit word is naari kera. While discussing some phonetic tendencies.' (https://www.valmikiRamayan.net/utf8/kish/sarga37/kishkindha_37_fRamae.htm)

There are some references of some divine fruits, tubers, and even the divine medicinal herbs these Vanars seen in the Himalayan region.

अत्र निस्यंद जातानि मूलानि च फलानि च |
अमृत स्वादु कल्पानि दद्दशुः तत्र वानराः || ४-३७-२९

There the vanara-s have seen luscious tubers and fruits similar to nectar, which have originated from the oblational food material spattered in the Vedic-ritual for Shiva.

तत् अत्र संभवम् दिव्यम् फलम् मूलम् मनोहरम् |
यः कश्चित् सकृत् अश्राति मासम् भवति तर्पितः || ४-३७-३०

If one eats for one time, a little of those divine and heart-pleasing fruits and tubers that have taken their origin from that oblational food material, he remains satiated for a month. [4-37-30]

तानि मूलानि दिव्यानि फलानि च फल अशनाः |
औषधानि च दिव्यानि जगृहुर् हरि पुंगवाः || ४-३७-३१

The best monkeys that are fruit-eaters have collected those divine fruits, tubers, and even the divine medicinal herbs. [4-37-31]

The mention of Rama instructing Nala about food and water supply highlights his leadership and strategic thinking—he ensured his massive army had enough resources for survival, which was crucial for the long journey to Lanka.

फल मूलवता नील शीत कानन वारिणा |
पथा मधुमता च आशु सेनाम् सेना पते नय || ६-४-१०

"Oh Nila the chief of Army! Steer the army speedily by the path,
abound with fruits and roots, cool woods and fresh water and honey."

त्रृषयेयुर् दुरात्मानः पथि मूल फल उदकम् || ६-४-११
राक्षसाः परिरक्षेथास् तेभ्यस् त्वम् नित्यम् उद्यतः |

"The evil-minded demons may spoil the roots, fruits and water in the
pathway. You always try to be on you guard."

Valmiki rishi clearly mentioned fruits, roots and honey while describing the march of Vanar sena to Lanka.

भक्षयन्तः सुगन्धीनि मधूनि च फलानि च || ६-४-२७
उद्वहन्तो महावृक्षान् मन्जरी पुन्ज धारिणः |

They marched on, eating good-smelling honeys and fruits and
carrying large branches bearing clusters of blossoms in multitude.

फलानि अमृत गन्धीनि मूलानि कुसुमानि च |
बुभुजुर् वानरास् तत्र पादपानाम् बल उत्कटाः || ६-४-९०

Monkeys in mad rut plucked sweet-smelling fruits,
roots, and flowers there.

द्रोण मात्र प्रमाणानि लम्बमानानि वानराः |
ययुः पिबन्तो हृष्टास् ते मधूनि मधु पिन्गलाः || ६-४-९१

Those monkeys, in reddish brown colour like honey, drinking honey
from honey-combs weighing about a maund each, went on cheerfully.

This shows that the Vanar Sena's diet in the *Ramayana* aligns with their nature as forest dwellers, relying on fruits, roots, and honey. Rama shown his leadership and strategic thinkin as he ensured his massive army had enough resources for survival, which was crucial for the long journey to Lanka.

Ravana's Private Bar: Pan Bhoomi and Exotic Delicacies

Ravana's Private Bar:
Pan Bhoomi and Exotic Delicacies

I began reading the *Sundar Kand* in search of references to food. Initially, I was somewhat sceptical about finding such references in this chapter. My understanding of the *Sundar Kand* had always been that it primarily highlights Hanuman's incredible deeds, his glory, and his tireless efforts to locate Sita. To my amazement, however, I discovered several references to food interwoven into the narrative.

One particularly vivid reference occurs when Hanuman enters the city of Lanka and searches its various buildings and landmarks. Most of his exploration is conducted at night, a deliberate strategy to maintain secrecy.

Assuming his *Sukshma Rupa* (a diminutive form), Hanuman infiltrates Ravana's palaces. Valmiki masterfully depicts the opulent interiors of Ravana's residences in this section. As Hanuman moves from one place to another, the descriptions evoke an image akin to modern drone footage, offering readers a sweeping and dynamic perspective of the grandeur of Lanka.

During one of his flights into Ravana's palace, Hanuman entered the opulent *Paan Bhoomi*—a grand bar within the wealthy palace. This bar was a haven of indulgence, filled with every desirable luxury. The scene was radiant, as though glowing without the presence of fire. Couches and chairs were meticulously arranged throughout the space, while the floor sparkled with garlands of flowers in varied patterns. Scattered across the room were golden and crystal vessels, many of which held smaller, intricately crafted golden containers.

Hanuman observed an array of delicacies and meats, each carefully arranged. He saw venison and buffalo meat, wild boar, and half-eaten peacocks and chickens. Meat from pigs and goats had been preserved in curd and seasoned with rock salt. There were exotic birds, such as *Krakara*, prepared in multiple styles, and *Chakora* birds, some partially eaten. Wild buffalo and fish, including the *Ekashleya*, were also present. Additionally, Hanuman noticed a variety of dishes to be licked, beverages, and other exquisite foods.

The floor itself was a remarkable sight, adorned with remnants of rich dishes and beverages. Musical instruments, necklaces, anklets, and armlets of immense value lay scattered amidst the display of indulgence. Some areas were covered with fruits left inside drinking vessels, while others were sprinkled with fragrant flowers. The meats were seasoned with the finest spices and sauces—sour, salty, and flavourful—and arranged separately with great care.

Hanuman's attention turned to the abundance of liquor stored in silver and golden vessels, many of them encrusted with gemstones. The bar held a variety of clear and excellent liquors, including *Sura* (a traditional alcoholic beverage), liquors made from sugar, honey, flowers, and fruits, as well as artificially crafted drinks. Each type was carefully prepared and infused with fragrant powders. He observed vessels of golden hues filled to varying levels—some completely full, some half-empty, and others entirely consumed.

As he explored further, Hanuman noticed remnants of rice and cooked food left scattered across the area. In some places, vessels were broken or overturned, while in others, pots lay in disarray. Pools of water mingled with garlands and fruits, creating a chaotic yet mesmerizing scene.

This description is so fascinating that it feels that you are watching a clip from a modern-day drone camara.

सर्व कामैर् उपेताम् च पान भूमिम् महात्मनः || ५-११-१०

ददर्श कपि शार्द्दूलः तस्य रक्षः पतेर् गृहे |

paanabhuumim cha = a bar also.

The best among Vanaras saw in that wealthy Ravana's house a bar also, consisting of all desirables.

मृगाणाम् महिषाणाम् च वराहाणाम् च भागशः || ५-११-११
तत्र न्यस्तानि मांसानि पान भूमौ ददर्श सः |

Hanuman saw there in that bar, meat of dear and of buffalo, of wild boar kept separately.

रौक्मेषु च विशलेषु भाजनेष्व् अर्ध भक्षितान् || ५-११-१२
ददर्श कपि शार्द्रूल मयूरान् कुक्कुटामः तथा |

The best among Vanaras saw half eaten peacocks and chicken in wide vessels of golden colour.

वराह वार्ध्राणिसकान् दधि सौवर्चल आयुतान् || ५-११-१३
शल्यान् म्ग मयूरामः च हनूमान् अन्ववैक्षत |

Hanuma observed meat of pigs and goats, porcupines, deer, and peacocks preserved in curds and sochal salt.

कृकरान् विविधान् सिद्धामः चकोरान् अर्ध भक्षितान् || ५-११-१४
महिषान् एक शल्यामः च चागामः च कृत निष्ठितान् |
लेख्यम् उच्च अवचम् पेयम् भोज्यानि विविधानि च || ५-११-१५

Hanuman saw birds called Krakara cooked ready to be eaten in variety of ways, birds called Chakoras half-eaten, wild buffalos, fishes called ekashleya, goats, food to be licked of various kinds, beverages, and various foods.

तथा अम्ल लवण उत्तंसैर् विविधै राग षाडवैः |
हार नूपुर केयूरैर् अपविद्धैर् महा धनैः || ५-११-१६
पान भाजन विक्षिप्तैः फलैः च विविधैर् अपि |
कृत पुष्प उपहारा भूर् अधिकम् पुष्यति श्रियम् || ५-११-१७

In the same way that floor was obtaining glory greatly with Ragas and Shadabas seasoned with sour and salty sauces, with necklaces, anklets and armlets of great value thrown around, with various fruits left in drinking vessels, with flowers sprinkled.

तत्र तत्र च विन्यस्तैः सुश्लिष्टैः शयन आसनैः |
पान भूमिर् विना वह्निम् प्रदीप्ता इव उपलक्ष्यते || ५-११-१८

That bar was seen as though radiant without fire, with couches and chairs well-arranged and placed there and there.

बहु प्रकारैर् विविधैर् वर संस्कार संस्कृतैः |
मांसैः कुशल सम्युक्तैः पान भूमि गतैः पृथक् || ५-११-१९

Many meats of different kinds cultured with various best seasonings, well-arranged separately obtained that bar.

दिव्याः प्रसन्ना विविधाः सुराः कृत सुरा अपि |
शर्कर आसव माध्वीकाः पुष्प आसव फल आसवाः || ५-११-२०
वास चूर्णैः च विविधैर् मृष्टाः तैः तैः पृथक् पृथक् |

Excellent and clear various liquors, a liquor called Sura, liquor made of sugar, liquor made of honey, liquor made of flowers and liquors made of fruits also, artificially made liquors - those and those were cultured separately with various fragrant powders.

सम्तता शुशुभे भूमिर् माल्यैः च बहु संस्थितैः || ५-११-२१
हिरण्मयैः च करकैर् भाजनैः स्फाटिकैर् अपि |
जाम्बूनदमयैश्चान्याः करकैरभिवम्वृता || ५-११-२२

The floor shone filled by flower garlands in a variety of forms, with various vessels of golden hue and also made of crystal, filled with other small vessels of golden colour.

राजतेषु च कुम्भेषु जाम्बूनदमयेषु च |
पान श्रेष्ठम् तदा भूरि कपिः तत्र ददर्श ह || ५-११-२३

*Hanuma saw indeed then lot of best quality liquor
in pots of silver and of golden colour.*

सो अपश्यत् शात कुम्भानि शीधोर् मणिमयानि च |
राजतानि च पूर्णानि भाजनानि महा कपिः || ५-११-२४

*That great Hanuman saw vessels full of liquor of golden colour,
embedded with gemstones and also of silver hue.*

क्वचिद् अर्ध अवशेषाणि क्वचित् पीतानि सर्वशः |
क्वचिन् न एव प्रपीतानि पानानि स ददर्श ह || ५-११-२५

*Hanuman saw indeed at some places drinks half-filled and at some
places completely drunk and some places not at all drunk.*

क्वचिद् भक्ष्यामः च विविधान् क्वचित् पानानि भागशः |
क्वचिद् अन्न अवशेषाणि पश्यन् वै विचचार ह || ५-११-२६

*Hanuman paced about seeing at some places various eatables and
at some places drinks separately, and at some places remnants of
cooked rice.*

क्वचित् प्रभिन्नैः करकैः क्वचिद् आलोडितैर् घटैः |
क्वचित् सम्पृक्त माल्यानि जलानि च फलानि च || ५-११-२७

*Hanuma saw some places with vessels broken,
some places with pots in shambles, some places with water together
with flower garlands and fruits.*

After reading these descriptions, we can imagine that Ravana's private bar is almost similar to modern day bars. It is full of all luxuries, foods, liquors, meats, and pleasures.

Kumbhkarna's Epic Diet

Kumbhkarna's Epic Diet

Kumbhakarna, the mighty Rakshasa warrior and younger brother of Ravana in the *Ramayan*, was known for his enormous size, incredible strength, and insatiable appetite. His diet, as described in various retellings and interpretations of the epic, was astonishingly vast, reflecting his gigantic physique and immense energy needs.

Kumbhakarna was cursed to sleep for six months at a time, waking up only for a single day before returning to slumber. On the day he woke up, his hunger was so immense that he would consume a massive quantity of food to sustain himself for the next six months of sleep.

According to the *Ramayana*, When Ravana woke Kumbhakarna to fight against Shree Rama, the Rakshasa was first offered a grand feast to restore his energy after months of sleep. This feast is described as consisting of:

Mountains of Rice and Grains: Kumbhakarna required vast amounts of rice, wheat, and other grains to satisfy his hunger.

ततश्चक्रुर्महात्मानः कुम्भकर्णस्य चाग्रातः ॥ ६-६०-३०
भूतानाम् मेरुसम्काशम् राशिम् परमतर्पणम् ।

Then, those powerful demons, in order to satisfy him, placed a heap of venison as high as Mount Meru, in front of Kumbhakarna.

Large quantities of Liquor and energy drinks: He was known to drink large quantities of *madira* (intoxicating drinks), equivalent to entire lakes or rivers of alcohol.

ततस्ते त्वरितास्तत्र राक्षसा रावणाज्ञया |
मद्यम् भक्ष्यांश्च विविधान् क्षिप्रमेवोपहारयन् || ६-६०-९१

Thereupon, those demons brought him quickly the wine and various kinds of eatable there, in their hurry to take Kumbhakarna with them as per Ravana's commands.

आदद्भुक्षितो मांसम् शोणितम् तृषितोऽपिबत् |
मेदःकुम्भांश्च मद्यांश्च पपौ शक्ररिपुस्तदा || ६-६०-६२

Then, the hungry Kumbhakarna, the enemy of Indra, ate the meat and being thirsty drank the blood and gulped pitchers full of fat and wine.

Kumbhakarna's diet included various energy drinks.

प्रक्षाल्य वदनम् हृ^ष्टः स्नातः परमभूषितः |
पिपासुस्त्वरयामास पानम् बलसमीरणम् || ६-६०-९०

Washing his face and bathing, refreshed, and delighted, adorning himself well and feeling thirsty, he hastened them to bring him a drink which can boost up his strength.

पीत्वा घटसहस्रे द्वे गमनायोपचक्रमे |
ईषत्समुत्कटो मत्तस्तेजोबलसमन्वितः || ६-६०-९२

Having drunk two thousand pitchers, Kumbhakarna prepared to set out and slightly inebriated and flushed, he was exhilarated and filled with energy.

Various Animals in huge quantity: He would devour whole animals, including buffaloes, deer, wild boars, and other creatures in massive quantities.

मृगाणाम् महिषाणाम् च वराहाणाम् च संचयान् || ६-६०-३१
चक्रुर्नैर्ऋतशार्द्रूला राशिमन्त्रस्य चाद्रतम् |

Those excellent demons piled up a great mass of wonderful food with the meat of deers, buffaloes and pigs.

ततः शोणितकुम्भांश्च मांसानि विविधानि च || ६-६०-३२
पुरस्तात्कुम्भकर्णस्य चक्रुस्त्रिदशशात्रवः |

Then, the demons placed pots of blood and various kinds of meat in front of Kumbhakarna.

ततस्त्वदर्शयन् सर्वान् भक्ष्यांश्च विविधान् बहून् |
वराहान् महिषांश्चैव बभक्ष स महाबलः || ६-६०-६१

Then, the demons pointed to various kinds of victuals, boar, and buffalo. The mighty Kumbhakarna devoured them.

Kumbhakarna Monstrous Appetite of demons, devils, bears and Vanars:

Kumbhkarna unleashes his immense power and speaks with great confidence, promising to annihilate Rama's forces. His declaration about satiating the demons with monkey flesh and drinking Rama and Lakshmana's blood is an example of his warlike bravado. Below shloka cannot be considered with its literal meaning. It should be considered as Kumbhakarn's self-exaggeration about his powers and his try to moral boost to Ravana.

राक्षसांस्तर्पयिष्यामि हरीणाम् मांसशोणितैः |
रामलक्ष्मणयोश्चापि स्वयम् पास्यामि शोणितम् || ६-६०-७९

"I shall satiate the demons with the flesh and blood of monkeys and, as for Rama and Lakshmana, I shall drink their blood myself."

The Epic mention that he also ate demons, devils (rasksha), Vanars as part of his demonic nature, there are multiple references when he was fighting the war with Vanar sena.

बुभुक्षितः शोणितमांसगृध्नु |प्रविश्य तद्वानरसैन्यमुग्रम् |
चखाद रक्षांसि हरीन्पिशाचान् |ऋक्षांश्च मोहाद्रधि कुम्भकर्णः |
यथैव मृत्युर्हरते युगान्ते |स भक्षयामास हरींश्च मुख्यान् || ६-६७-९५

Penetrating that huge army of monkeys, Kumbhakarna who was greedily desirous of flesh and blood in hunger, due to his deep bewilderment in battle, ate away even the demons, monkeys, devils, and bears. He devoured the principal monkeys just as the death devours people at the time of the end of the world.

एकम् द्वौ त्रीन् बहून् क्रुद्धो वानरान् सह राक्षसैः |
समादायैकहस्तेन प्रचिक्षेप त्वरन्मुखे || ६-६७-९६

The enraged Kumbhakarna, quickly taking with his single hand, the monkeys, and demons, in one's two's, three's or in many and hurled them into his mouth

सम्प्रस्रवंस्तदा मेदः शोणित च महाबलः |
वध्यमानो नगेन्द्राग्रैर्भक्षयामास वानरान् || ६-६७-९७

Struck with mountain-peaks, by the monkeys, the mighty Kumbhakarna, then, gushing forth his flesh and blood, devoured the monkeys.

ते भक्ष्यमाणा हरयो रामम् जग्मुस्तदा गतिम् |
कुम्भकर्णो भृशम् क्रुद्धः कपीन् खादन् प्रधावति || ६-६७-९८

Thereupon, those monkeys, who were being devoured, sought Rama as their refuge. The very much enraged Kumbhakarna, while eating away the monkeys, marched forward.

शतानि सप्त चाष्टौ च विंशत्लिंशत्तथैव च |
सम्परिष्वज्य बहुभ्याम् खादन्विपरिधावति || ६-६७-९९

Grasping a hundred, a seven, an eight, a twenty and a thirty with his arms, Kumbhakarna was devouring the monkeys and running about in the battle-field.

Kumbhakarna's massive diet symbolizes the indulgence and the excessive nature of Rakshasas. His ability to consume such vast quantities shows his immense physical power. His lifestyle of prolonged sleep followed by excessive feasting signifies imbalance, a contrast to the disciplined way of life promoted in dharmic traditions.

Kumbhakarna's diet, as described in the *Ramayana*, is one of the most fascinating aspects of his character. His voracious appetite was both a source of humour and horror, portraying him as a force of nature that required extraordinary sustenance to function. This depiction adds to his legendary status as one of the most formidable warriors in Ravana's army.

The Duality of Visha (Poison) and Amrut (Nectar or Elixir)

The Duality of Visha (Poison) and Amrut (Nectar or Elixir)

Valmiki Ramayana, two significant concepts—*Visha* (poison) and *Amrut* (nectar or elixir)—are referenced, symbolizing opposing forces with profound implications in both spiritual and material contexts. Although these two concepts are not directly comparable or considered as Food or eatables both are commonly used in India present day India also.

The legend of churning Milk Ocean is narrated to Rama and Lakshmana when they reach and see a city named Vishaala. Vishvamitra narrates how haalaahala, the lethal poison as well as Amrita, the ambrosial elixir emerged from the churning of Milk Ocean, and how Shiva contained the poison and how Vishnu helped the churning in His incarnation as Tortoise.

Visha (Poison): *Visha*, often associated with harmful substances or poisons, appears throughout the *Ramayana* in various forms. One of the most notable instances is during the conflict between the forces of good, led by Shree Rama, and the forces of evil, led by Ravana. The use of poison can be seen symbolically as a force that corrupts and destroys life, representing the negative and destructive tendencies of the mind. It also signifies the ill effects of pride, anger, and hatred—emotions that can poison the mind and impede spiritual progress.

उत्पपाताग्निसंकाशं हालाहलमहाविषम् |
तेन दग्धं जगत्सर्वं सदेवासुरमानुषम् || १-४५-२०

A lethal poison similar to inferno known as haalaahala has started to fulminate therefrom, by which whole universe of gods, non-gods and humans is burnt down.

इत्युक्त्वा च सुरश्रेष्ठस्तत्रैवान्तरधीयत |
देवतानां भयं दृष्ट्वा श्रुत्वा वाक्यं तु शार्ङ्गिणः || १-४५-२५
हालाहलं विषं घोरं संजग्राहामृतोपमम् |

Saying so Vishnu, the best one among gods, has disappeared then and there only. And on observing the scare of gods and also on paying heed to the words of the Wielder of Bow called shaar~Nga, namely Vishnu, god Shiva gulped that lethal poison, haalaahala, as if it is ambrosia.

During the conversation between King Dasharath and Kausalya, Dashrath mentions poison many times pointing out the destructive element in Kaikai's demands to send Rama to exile.

तत् इदम् मे अनुसम्प्राप्तम् देवि दुह्खम् स्वयम् कृतम् |
सम्मोहात् इह बालेन यथा स्यात् भक्षितम् विषम् || २-६३-१२

"This grief, obtained by my own accord, has befallen me, as by a boy in ignorance eating poison in the world; O, Kausalya!"

Describing the condition of capital city of Ayodhya after Rama, Laxman and Sita went to exile, Valmiki says the city was shunned like poisoned food.

अप्रहृष्ट बलाम् न्यूनाम् विषमस्थाम् अनावृताम् |
शत्रवो न अभिमन्यन्ते भक्ष्यान् विष कृतान् इव || २-८८-२५

City-gates laid open, without any defenders, denuded of its happy army, plunged in desolation in difficulties and exposed, that royal capital of Ayodhya will be shunned like poisoned food even by the enemies.

The episode involving the *Visha* in the *Ramayana* where Ravana's sister, Shurpanakha, is wounded by Lakshmana and later uses poison in an attempt to harm Sita, further exemplifies the harmful nature of *Visha*. This destructive element is in direct contrast to the healing and life–sustaining qualities of *Amrut*.

Amrut (Nectar or Elixir): *Amrut*, in the *Ramayana*, is often regarded as the divine nectar of immortality, a substance that has the power to grant eternal life and supreme wisdom. It represents the positive, life-affirming aspects of the universe. In the *Ramayana*, *Amrut* can be seen symbolically as the spiritual sustenance that nourishes the soul and helps one achieve enlightenment. The concept of *Amrut* is closely linked to the divine grace of Shree Vishnu (Rama) and the righteousness he upholds.

The concept of *Amrut* also has parallels in the story of Ravana's quest for immortality. Despite his knowledge of divine nectar and his desire for eternal life, Ravana's arrogance and pride ultimately lead him to his downfall. This illustrates that while *Amrut* has the potential to elevate the soul, it is available only to those who follow the path of righteousness and humility.

In a broader philosophical sense, *Amrut* signifies purity, wisdom, and divine favor, contrasting sharply with the destructive, corrupting nature of *Visha*. Together, they highlight the dual nature of existence—where the choice between good and evil, purity and corruption, lies at the heart of human experience.

यन् मन्गलम् सुपर्णस्य विनता अकल्पयत् पुरा || २-२५-३३
अमृतम् प्रार्थयानस्य तत् ते भवतु मन्गलम् |

"Which blessing was invoked by Vinata to Garuda who was setting off to bring nectar in the past, may that blessing happen to you."

नीचस्य क्षुद्र शीलस्य मिथ्या वृत्तस्य रक्षसः |
प्राणान् अपहरिष्यामि गरुत्मान् अमृतम् यथा || ३-३०-५

"In boasting you are knavish, in character roguish, and in behaviour ghoulish, such a demon as you are, I will take your life away as the Divine Eagle Garuda took away Ambrosia. [3-30-5]"

Significance of Wines and Liquors

Significance of Wines and Liquors

Ramayana contains several references to wine (madira) and other alcoholic beverages. These references generally appear in contexts related to royal luxury, celebrations, and sometimes indulgence. Below are some key instances where wine or alcohol is mentioned in the *Ramayana*:

Royal Banquets and Celebrations

In several instances, kings and warriors are described as enjoying quality food and drinks. Royal courts and gatherings included alcoholic beverages as part of the feasting culture.

Kaikeyi's chamber is described as having luxurious surroundings, including wine and intoxicating drinks. There is a conversation between king Dasarath and Kaikeyi

After hearing the cruel words of Kaikeyi, Dasharath exclaimed with anguish,

सतीम् त्वामहमत्यन्तम् व्यवस्याम्यसतीम् सतीम् || २-१२-७६
रूपिणीम् विषसम्युक्ताम् पीत्वेव मदिराम् नरह् |

"I considered you a good and virtuous wife, yet you reveal yourself to be like one who has consumed wine (madira) laced with poison (visha)—deceptively sweet, but ultimately lethal.

The metaphor of "wine and poison" here is not just poetic; it draws upon ancient cultural symbolism. In many traditions, wine often symbolizes celebration or truth, while poison represents betrayal or destruction. The duality reflects the bitter irony of trust turned to treachery.

Later when Rama, Laxman and Sita went for exile. They had to cross the river Ganga with the help of Guha the Nishadraj (The king of Nishadh). Sita prayed to the river Ganga and she mentioned the offerings, including meat, in lieu of Rama's safe return from his exile. Interestingly here the meat and wines both are mentioned.

सुराघटसहस्रेण मांसभूतोदनेन च |
यक्ष्ये त्वाम् प्रयता देवि पुरीम् पुनरुपागता || २-५२-८९

"Oh, goddess! After reaching back the city of Ayodhya, I shall worship you with thousand pots of spirituous liquor and jellied meat with cooked rice well prepared for the solemn rite."

Indulgence of Rakshasas (Demons)

The rakshasas (demons), especially those in Lanka under Ravana, are often depicted indulging in wine. There is separate chapter in this book describing the abundance in Ravana's palace. (Chapter–Ravana's private Bar Pan Boomi). Ravana's palace is described as having an abundance of intoxicating drinks.

Ravana seen to be consuming wine in the epic, there are several references pointing towards this. When Hanuman enters into Ravan's palace, he found that the king is in sleep on a shining couch resting after drinking.

पीत्वा अपि उपरतम् च अपि ददर्श स महा कपिः |
भास्करे शयने वीरम् प्रसुप्तम् राक्षस अधिपम् || ५-१०-११

That great Hanuma saw the gallant king of rakshasas in sleep on a shining couch resting after drinking.

Yuddha Kanda (the Book of War) of the *Ramayana*, there are instances where some of the Ravana's warriors urge him to relax, indulge in wine, and entrust them with the responsibility of fighting the war. Prahasta the army chief of Ravana and Kumbhakarna both mention the same sentences. This highlights not only the rakshasa (demonic) culture of indulgence and overconfidence.

रमस्व कामम् पिब चाग्र्यवारुणीम् |कुरुष्व कार्वाणि हितानि विज्वरः |
मया तु रामे गमिते यमक्षयम् |चिराय सीता वशगा भविष्यति || ६-१२-४०

"Enjoy yourself freely. Drink excellent of wines to the extent of your desire without any anxiety. Rama, having been dispatched by me to the abode of death, Sita will be at your disposal forever."

"O king! You make merry today and drink wine. Throw away your agony and perform your usual duties. While I send Rama to death

Ravana's brother Kumbhakarna described to consume plenty of wine and other liquors. The chapter **Kumbhkarna's Diet** in this book describe in detail. After battles or victories, rakshasas are described as drinking wine in celebration.

Celebratory Drinking by Vanaras (Monkey Warriors)

After the victory over Ravana, the Vanaras (monkey warriors) celebrate with feasting and drinking. Sugriva, the king of the Vanaras, is particularly noted for his love of wine and indulgence. Before meeting Rama, Sugriva is initially found in a drunken state, indulging in wine and merriment.

Laxman mentions comments below to Tara, when he entered into Kiskindha to remind the promise and duties of Sugreev. Here he is mentioning about dunked Sugreev.

न हि धर्मार्थ सिद्ध्यर्थम् पानम् एवम् प्रशस्यते ।
पानात् अर्थस्य कामः च धर्मः च परिहीयते ॥ ४-३३-४६

"For the purpose of achieving rightly rectitude and rightful riches this way of bacchanalia is inappreciable, isn't it! Just going on drinking will bring prosperity, aspirations and even probity to ruin.

Valmiki mentions that even the Vidyadhara(s) also drinks wine. Vidyādhara, meaning "wisdom-holders" are a group of supernatural beings who possess magical powers. They also attend Shiva, are considered Upadevas, or demi-gods. During Hanuman's flight over the sea to Lanka, Vidyadharas got surprised and shocked with acts of Hanuman. Things are described as below.

भिद्यतेऽयं गिरिर्भूतैरिति मत्त्वा तपस्विनः ।
त्रस्ता विद्याधरास्तस्मादुत्पेतुः स्त्रीगणैः सह॥ ५-१-२२
पानभूमिगतं हित्वा हैममासवभाजनम् ।
पात्राणि च महार्हाणि करकांश्च हिरण्मयान् ॥५-१-२३
लेह्यानुच्चावचान् भक्ष्यान् मांसानि विविधानि च ।
आर्षभाणि च चर्माणि खड्गांश्च कनकत्सरून् ॥ ५-१-२४

Ascetics residing on that mountain flew away from there thinking that some demons were destroying it. Vidhyadharas who lived there, became afraid, and flew away with their women folk, leaving behind them golden jugs of wine in the liquor house, gold vases, a variety of sauces that can be licked, eatables, various meats, skins of oxen and swords with golden hilts.

Wine as a Symbol of Pleasure, hospitality, and Decadence

One such description is given in this book under the chapter 'Sage Vashistha and the wish-fulfilling cow, Shabala- Vashishta's Feast.'

In the Balkand of the epic, it is mentioned that the holy cow Shabala arranges the wine for the army along with other food stuffs.

In another similar description in Aranya kand similar fest described. The sage Bharadwaj invokes the divine architect, Visvakarma, requesting him to prepare an extraordinary display of hospitality for Bharata and his companions. Bharadwaj says– 'Let some rivers flow with Maireya.' This is described in detail under the chapter 'Rishi Bharadwaj's feast to Bharata and his army.'

Notably, two revered sages, Vashishta and Bharadwaja, arrange elaborate feasts that include wine for their guests. This suggests that within the Framework of hospitality, such offerings were customary and widely accepted, even in ascetic settings. The presence of wine in these feasts indicates that it was not viewed as inherently inappropriate but rather as part of the broader social customs of the time.

On the other hand, in many places, alcohol is associated with pleasure, leisure, and sometimes moral decay. It is often seen in the context of royal indulgence or rakshasa hedonism.

The contrast between the disciplined, dharmic (righteous) life of Rama and the indulgent, decadent life of Ravana is subtly reflected in their differing attitudes toward wine.

In the *Ramayana*, wine is referenced mainly in royal and rakshasa contexts, often linked to luxury, indulgence, and sometimes excess. While it is not outright condemned, the epic subtly portrays excessive indulgence in alcohol as a characteristic of moral weakness, especially among the rakshasas and those who deviate from dharma. Characters like Rama and Sita uphold a life of discipline and virtue by abstaining from such indulgences, reinforcing the epic's moral themes.

The Significance of Soma (Somrus)

The Significance of Soma (Somrus)

Somras and wine are mostly gets confused by many. They use both words interchangeably; However, they are vastly different. Wine refers to intoxicating alcohol, which has no place in divine rituals.

In Hindu mythology, Soma (or Somras) is revered as a divine elixir, often described as the "nectar of the gods." It is believed to bestow immortality and unparalleled bliss upon those who consume it. Highly esteemed in the Vedas, Soma is depicted as a sacred plant whose extracted juice played a crucial role in sacrificial rituals, serving as a conduit between mortals and the divine realm.

Soma was a central offering in Vedic ceremonies, closely associated with Indra, the king of the gods, who is frequently described as drawing strength from its consumption. While the exact botanical identity of the Soma plant remains unknown, scholars have speculated on various possible species based on ancient textual descriptions.Beyond its literal consumption, Soma symbolizes spiritual enlightenment, purification, and divine connection, embodying the transcendental experience sought through Vedic rites.

Ther are few references of Soma or Somarus in the Valmiki *Ramayana*. This beverage is prepared from the stalks of soma plant. Soma creeper is from Sacrostemma Brevistigma of Asclepiadacea family, and some other scholars hold the view that it is from Sarcostema Viminalis family. In Vedic times, Soma was a plant given as an offering to the gods. There was great mysticism and spiritual power surrounding the plant. So much so that it was considered a deity in its own right leading many to search for the true identity of this revered plant.

At the time of Ashvamedha Yadnya King Dasharath perform a mid-day ritual where he squeezes the Soma juice.

ऐन्द्रश्च विधिवद्दत्तो राजा चाभिषुतोऽनघः |
माध्यंदिनं च सवनं प्रावर्तत यथाक्रमम् || १-१४-६

The oblations addressed to Indra are well given as ordained, and the flawless king Dasharatha also crushed the Soma creeper to squeeze Soma juice, and thus the mid-day savana ritual has come to pass according to sequence.

Kausalya, overcome with sorrow, reproaches Dasaratha for the grave injustice of exiling Rama. She vividly describes the hardships endured by Rama, Lakshmana, and Sita in the forest. Expressing her concerns, she questions whether Rama would even accept the throne upon his return in the fifteenth year, knowing that it had been ruled by Bharata.

Furthermore, she doubts that Bharata would willingly relinquish the kingdom and its treasury. She compares Rama's predicament to one who refuses nectar after its essence has been drained or to a sacrifice where only the remnants of the sacred Soma plant remain.

तथा हि आत्तम् इदम् राज्यम् हृत साराम् सुराम् इव |
न अभिमन्तुम् अलम् रामः नष्ट सोमम् इव अध्वरम् || २-६१-१८

"Thus, Rama cannot accept the kingdom taken away by other, as those not accepting an ambrosia whose essence has been taken away or as in a sacrifice, stalks of Soma plant (from which a beverage called Soma is prepared) are lost."

The Rakshasa's Diet

The Rakshasa's Diet

The epic *Ramayana*, the Rakshasas (demons or asuras) are depicted as powerful beings with varying food habits, often contrasting with the norms of dharma followed by humans (manavas) and divine beings (devas). Their dietary practices can be classified as follows:

Rakshasas are often described as Predominantly Carnivorous consuming meat, including human flesh. Many of them, especially those residing in the deep forests and remote regions, are portrayed as fearsome man-eaters.

अगस्त्यः परमामर्षस्ताटकामपि शप्तवान् || १-२५-१२
पुरुषादी महायक्षी विरूपा विकृतानना |
इदं रूपं विहायाशु दारुणं रूपमस्तु ते || १-२५-१३

"Highly infuriated sage Agastya even cursed Tataka saying, 'forthwith divested of this form of a beautiful female, oh, great yakshii, you shall become a man eater with your form distorted, face contorted, and shape monstrous.' [1-25-12b, 13]

Rama, Laxman, and Sita entered the Dandakaranya forest. Viradha the demon confronts Rama and other and tries to abduct Sita, and then Rama. Viradha the demon confronts Rama and other and tries to abduct Sita, and then Rama. The killing of this Viradha is the first act of Rama in eliminating negative forces in his empire to establish Rama Raajya. Viradha talked about himself referring his habits of eating human flesh and blood.

अहम् वनम् इदम् दुर्गम् विराधो नाम राक्षसः || ३-२-१२
चरामि सायुधो नित्यम् ऋषि मांसानि भक्षयन् |

"I am a demon named Viradha and I will be on the rove in this impassable forest with weapon, always eating the flesh of sages.

इयम् नारी वरारोहा मम भार्या भविष्यति || ३-२-१३
युवयोः पापयोः च अहम् पास्यामि रुधिरम् मृधे |

"This best waisted woman will be my wife, and I will drink your blood of you two sinful one in a fight with you.

There is a reference of Shurpnakha – Ravana's sister talking to Laxman that she shall eat Rama and Sita to make Laxman free to marry her.

इमाम् विरूपाम् असतीम् करालाम् निर्णत उदरीम् |
अनेन सह ते भ्रात्रा भक्षयिष्यामि मानुषीम् || ३-१७-२७

"Shall I eat up this disfigured, dishonest, diabolical human female with a hallow stomach along with him, that brother of yours to make you free.

Ravana and his demonic followers are said to enjoy grand feasts with meat and blood. Khara, Dushana, and Trishira, the Rakshasa commanders in Dandakaranya, are depicted as terrorizing sages and even devouring them. Kabandha, a Rakshasa cursed into a grotesque form, attempted to eat Rama and Lakshmana.

Some Rakshasas are portrayed as drinking blood and consuming intoxicating substances. They are described as reveling in feasts filled with flesh and wine, indulging in gluttonous behaviour. Ravana's court in Lanka is depicted as having lavish banquets with meat and strong alcoholic beverages.

Rakshasas in Lanka, particularly in Ravana's palace, followed elaborate rituals around their feasts, often involving sacrificial offerings and dark rites. They also engaged in ceremonial consumption of meat and wine during victories or festivals. This is described in detail separately in another chapter in this book.

Food habits of the giants like Kumbhakarna includes rice, wheat various meats like buffaloes, deer, wild boars, and other creatures along with drinks blood in massive quantities. There is a separate chapter describing his food habits in this book.

Similarly, there are references of the Rakshasa ladies talking to Sita to eat her. They were found talking amongst them that how will they distribute Sita's body parts to eat. These could be the tactics to threaten Sita and agree her to go with Ravana.

ततस्तु प्रघसा नाम राक्षसी वाक्यमब्रवीत् ।
कण्ठमस्या नृशंसायाः पीडयाम किमास्यते ॥ ५-२४-४२

An ogre woman named Pragasa spoke these words: "Squeeze the neck of this cruel woman. Why do we delay?"

निवेद्यतां ततो राज्ञे मानुषी सा मृतेति ह ।
नात्र कश्चन संदेहः खादतेति स वक्ष्यति ॥ ५-२४-४३

"Thereafter let it be known to the king that that human woman has died. He will say thus: "Eat.". There is no doubt in this matter."

ततस्त्वजामुखी नाम राक्षसी वाक्यमब्रवीत् |

विशस्येमां ततः सर्वाः समान् कुरुत पीलुकान् || ५-२४-४४

"Thereafter an ogre woman named Ajamukhi spoke these words: "All of you killing this woman thereafter do equal pieces."

विभजाम ततः सर्वा विवादो मे न रोचते |

पेयमानीयतां क्षिप्रं लेह्यमुच्चावचं बहु || ५-२४-४५

"Thereafter all of us will divide. Quarrel is not desirable to me. Liquor, many kinds and a lot of lickables be brought quickly."

Sita replied that they could freely eat her, but she will not listen to what they say.

न मानुषी राक्षसस्य भार्या भवितुमर्हति |

कामं खादत मां सर्वा न करिष्यामि वो वचः || ५-२४-८

"Human woman is not waited to become wife of an ogre. All of you freely eat me. I will not honour your words."

Some sages cursed into Rakshasa forms (like Maricha, before becoming Ravana's servant) initially lived ascetically, sustaining themselves on roots, fruits, and leaves.

Overall, the food habits of Rakshasas in the *Ramayana* largely reflected their aggressive, tamasic (dark and chaotic) nature. However, not all Rakshasas were inherently evil, and some followed disciplined, vegetarian, or dharmic diets.

Their dietary practices symbolized their moral alignment—those indulging in excessive violence and gluttony were often the antagonists, while those choosing restraint and dharma, like Vibhishana, were portrayed positively.

Edible Fruits and Roots in the Ramayana

Edible Fruits and Roots in the Ramayana

Rama, Laxman, and Sita spent their exile in various forests, including Chitrakuta, Dandaka-aranya, Panchavati, Kishkindha (Pampa Sarovar), and Lanka. Among these, Chitrakuta and Dandaka-aranya are dense, thick forests, while Panchavati is more accurately described as a sub-forest. The majority of the narrative unfolds in these forests, which is why this portion of the Ramayan is also referred to as the Aranya Kanda.

Valmiki employs three distinct terms to describe the forests encountered during their exile: *Vana*, *Aranya*, and *Vatika*. *Vana* refers to sub-forests that often include agricultural fields, such as Panchavati. *Aranya* signifies dense, untamed forests, exemplified by Chitrakuta, Dandaka, and Kishkindha. *Vatika* denotes groves or plantations that have undergone some human intervention, like the Ashoka Vatika. These forests were essential sources of sustenance—providing fruits, roots, and other edibles to Rama, Lakshmana, and Sita throughout their exile.

Chitrakuta Hills- During his exile, Shree Rama first sought the guidance of Sage Bharadwaja at Prayag (modern-day Prayagraj). Following the sage's counsel, he, along with Sita and Lakshmana, journeyed to the serene and resource-rich Chitrakuta forest. This picturesque region, renowned for its calmness and natural abundance, provided an ideal refuge for the exiled trio. Chitrakuta's verdant hills were adorned with a diverse array of fruit-bearing trees, ensuring a sustainable source of nourishment during their stay. Some edible plants/fruits from the list are as below:

Amra / Mango (*Mangifera indica*) – A widely known fruit, sweet and juicy.

Jamun / Indian black plum (*Syzygium cumini*) – A dark purple fruit, often used in jams, juices, and pickles.

Chironji / Almondette tree (*Buchanania lanzan*) – The seeds are edible and used in cooking.

Kathal / Jackfruit (*Artocarpus heterophyllus*) – A large fruit, known for its sweet and fibrous flesh, often used in savory dishes when unripe.

Bhavya / Dillenia (*Dillenia indica*) – Its fruit is edible and used for making juices and jams in some regions.

Bel / Bengal quince (*Aegle marmelos*) – The fruit is edible and used in various culinary preparations, especially in Ayurvedic remedies.

Tendu / Gaub persimmon (*Diospyros melanoxylon*) – The fruit of this tree is edible and commonly used in making local treats and dried products.

Mahua / Indian butter tree (*Madhuca longifolia var. latifolia*) – The flowers are edible and used in preparing sweet dishes and alcoholic beverages.

Ber / Indian jujube (*Zizyphus mauritiana*) – A small, sweet fruit often eaten fresh or dried.

Aonla / Indian Gooseberry (*Phyllanthus emblica*) – Known for its sour flavor, it is rich in vitamin C and used in pickles, juices, and Ayurvedic medicine.

Bijak / Pomegranate (*Punica granatum*) – The seeds are edible and consumed in several ways, including as fresh fruit or in juices.

Neebu / Bigarade Orange (*Citrus aurantifolia*) – Also known as lime, it is commonly used for its juice in beverages and cooking.

Dandaka Aranya & Panchvati Area- Later, they relocated to Dandaka Aranya, an expansive and dense forest spanning parts of present-day Madhya Pradesh, Odisha, and Andhra Pradesh. This ancient woodland was home to both revered sages and formidable Rakshasas (demons), creating a landscape of both spiritual significance and lurking perils. The name "Dandaka" is derived from a legendary demon king who, upon being cursed, transformed the forest into a land fraught with dangers and mystical challenges.

In the *Aranya Kanda*, the hermitages are described as "aranyaisca mahavriksaih punyaih sveduphalair vritam" (2.1.5), meaning they are surrounded by towering forest trees, sacred groves, and an abundance of sweet fruit-bearing trees. The forests mentioned in the text were rich in diverse flora, including significant plant species such as *Madhuka* (Indian butter tree), *Bilva* (Bengal quince), and *Badari* (Indian jujube) (4.11.74), all of which played an essential role in the region's natural and spiritual ecosystem.

The next significant stop in Shree Rama's exile was Panchavati, a serene and spiritually significant region situated on the banks of the River Godavari. It was here that Sita was abducted by Ravana, marking a pivotal moment in the Ramayan. Panchavati is also noted for its agricultural abundance, with references in ancient texts to various cereals such as *yava* (barley), corn, and wheat, highlighting the region's fertile landscape and self-sustaining environment.

बाष्प च्छहन्नानि अरण्यानि यव गोधूमवंति च |
शोभन्ते अभ्युदिते सूर्ये नदद्भिः क्रौन्च सारसैः || ४-१६-१६

"Covered with the dew the forests that already covered with crop fields of barley and wheat are beaming forth, together with the callings of waterfowls, at the rise of the sun.

There was a forested plain called samam which comprised of fruit yielding, flowery, aromatic and hardwood trees.

The region was home to a diverse range of tree species, including *Shala* (Sal tree), *Palmyra palm, Tamala* (West Indian Bay tree), *Date palm, Jackfruit, Punnaga* (Alexandrian laurel), *Sweet mango,* and *Tilaka* (Sesame). Additionally, the sacred *Tulsi* (Holy Basil) and the aquatic *Lotus* were found in abundance, further enhancing the area's spiritual and ecological richness (*Aranya Kanda* 3.5.11). References to agricultural produce such as *Yava* (barley), wheat, and *Śāli* (winter rice) indicate that the region was not only rich in natural flora but also supported staple food crops essential for sustenance.

Pampa Sarovar & Kishkindha- During their search for Sita, Rama and Lakshmana encountered the demon Kabandha, who, upon being vanquished, guided them westward toward Pampa Sarovar and Kishkindha. Pampa Sarovar, a sacred lake nestled between the Rishyamukha Hill to the west and Matanga Hill to the east, continues to be recognized by its ancient names.

This historically and spiritually significant site is located in the present-day Bellari district of Karnataka, where the revered Pampa Sarovar remains a place of pilgrimage. Kishkindha, the kingdom of the Vanaras (monkey warriors), played a crucial role in Rama's journey, as it was here that he formed an alliance with Hanuman and Sugriva, setting the stage for the eventual battle against Ravana.

The *Ramayan* highlights the rich biodiversity of the regions Shree Rama and his companions traversed, emphasizing the variety and purity of the flora, fauna, and water sources. The vegetation in these areas was primarily of the dry and moist deciduous type, providing an abundant and diverse ecosystem. The forests were home to numerous fruit-bearing species, including *Jambu* (rose apple), *Priyala* (Almondette tree), *Banyan*, *Plaksha* (Indian fig), *Panasa* (jackfruit), *Amra* (mango), *Vanjula* (rattan cane), and *Ciribilva* (Bengal quince).

Additionally, the landscape featured a lush and pristine *Vana* (forest), resembling those in heavenly realms. The beauty of the region was further enhanced by the presence of full-bloomed lotuses, lilies, and *Padmaka* (Himalayan wild cherry), contributing to the serene atmosphere of the sacred Pampa Sarovar (lake).

As Rama and Lakshmana wandered through the forest in search of Sita, they encountered a *Badari* (Indian jujube) tree. In their distress, they asked the tree if it had seen Sita passing by. To their relief, the tree responded affirmatively and indicated the direction in which she had gone. Grateful for the tree's assistance, Rama, deeply moved by its gesture, blessed the tree with a boon, ensuring that it would remain immortal and never perish, regardless of the circumstances. This act of kindness reflected Rama's deep connection to nature and his reverence for all living beings.

In another incident during his exile, Rama encountered **Sabari**, a humble tribal woman who was a devoted follower of his. She offered few fruits to Rama and Laxman. Rama's acceptance of the simple fruit, offered with such devotion, elevated it to a revered status. Although this incident is not mentioned in the detail in Valmiki *Ramayana*, Valmiki just says Sabari offered some fruits to Rama and Laxman. There is no mention of any specific fruit.

Forest of Lanka Edible plants in Ashoka vatika

No major differences can be distinguished between the tropical deciduous forests and the evergreen Lankan forest also known as green wood. The two main characteristics of the Lankan forests are the natural and the naturalized forests.

Valmiki's detailed account in the *Ramayan* presents a vivid description of both edible and non-edible vegetation, including *Mango*, *Beal* (Bengal quince), *Jackfruit*, *Jujube*, *Myrobalan*, and a type of sour fruit called *Bhavya* (Dillenia). Other notable species described in the text include *Campaka* (Champak), *Chandana* (Sandalwood tree), *Nagakesara* (Cobras saffron, Ironwood tree), *Sala* (Sal tree), *Uddalaka* (Indian Cherry), and various *Mango* groves (*5.5.43, 38; 5.15.2, 3,115*).

The *Ramayan* also references the Sleshmaataka (Indian Cherry) forest, known as *Sleshmaataka Vana*, located around Gokarna, where Shree Shiva once concealed himself in the form of a stag. Furthermore, the epic mentions the use of Sleshmaataka wood in the construction of wooden ritual posts, adhering to specific ceremonial guidelines (*1.14.22-23*), underscoring the sacred and ritualistic significance of the Indian Cherry in Vedic traditions.

All these descriptions of various forest plants provide valuable material for primary research. The Valmiki *Ramayana* serves as a remarkable resource for students and researchers in the fields of Agriculture, Horticulture, Food Science, and Ayurvedic Medicine, offering insights into ancient botanical knowledge and traditional practices. It is a testament to the rich biodiversity of ancient India's forests, reflecting a time when human civilization thrived in harmony with nature.

The depth of ecological awareness in the epic highlights the sustainable relationship between people and their environment, inspiring modern research and conservation efforts.

Medicinal Plants oils and preservation techniques

Medicinal Plants Oils and Preservation Techniques

Although medicinal plants and oils are not traditionally classified as **"foods,"** many of them are consumed for their therapeutic effects. Given their significant role in health and well-being, I felt it was essential to preserve this wealth of knowledge. Therefore, I have included them in this book to highlight their relevance and contribution to ancient dietary and medicinal practices.

The description in *Ramayana* indicates that people of that era possessed knowledge of preserving bodies using medicinal oils. It also suggests they had advanced techniques for extracting and preparing such oils, showcasing their understanding of preservation and medicinal practices.

When Rama and Laxman went into exile, and King Dasharath passed away, Bharat and Shatrughan were at their uncle's residence and could not return immediately. During this period, the preservation of King Dasharath's body became essential. Ancient texts mention that, following the instructions of Guru Vashishtha, the king's body was placed in a tub of oil for 8–10 days until Bharat returned to perform the *antya sanskar* (last rites).

तैल द्रोण्याम् अथ अमात्याः सम्वेश्य जगती पतिम् ।
राज्ञः सर्वाणि अथ आदिष्टाः चक्रुः कर्माणि अनन्तरम् ॥ २-६६-१४

The ministers assigned for the job kept the king in an oil trough and did all the acts that were to be done thereafter.

न तु सम्कलनम् राज्ञो विना पुत्रेण मन्त्रिणः ।
सर्वज्ञाः कर्तुम् ईषुस् ते ततः रक्षन्ति भूमिपम् ॥ २-६६-१५

The ministers who were knowing all such matters were not willing to do cremation for the king in the absence of his sons and that is why preserved the king's body. (in an oil through).

तैल द्रोण्याम् तु सचिवैः शायितम् तम् नर अधिपम् |
हा मृतः अयम् इति ज्ञात्वा स्त्रियः ताः पर्यदेवयन् || २-६६-१६

Seeing that the king was laid down in an oil through by the ministers those women in the gynaacium cried "Alas! He is dead!"

उद्धृतम् तैल सम्क्लेदात् स तु भूमौ निवेशितम् |
आपीत वर्ण वदनम् प्रसुप्तम् इव भूमिपम् || २-७६-४
सम्वेश्य शयने च अग्र्ये नाना रत्न परिष्कृते |
ततः दशरथम् पुत्रः विललाप सुदुह्खितः || २-७६-५

Raising the body of king Dasaratha, from the vessel where it had been immersed in oil, seeming as it were asleep with face in the colour of gold, that son Bharata placed it in a magnificent couch, adorned with every kind of precious stone and in a great grief, lamented.

From the Himalayan alpine region

There are some references of some divine fruits, tubers, and even the divine medicinal herbs these Vanars seen in the Himalayan region.

अत्र निस्यंद जातानि मूलानि च फलानि च |
अमृत स्वादु कल्पानि ददृशुः तत्र वानराः || ४-३७-२९

There the vanara-s have seen luscious tubers and fruits similar to nectar, which have originated from the oblational food material spattered in the Vedic-ritual for Shiva.

तत् अन्न संभवम् दिव्यम् फलम् मूलम् मनोहरम् ।
यः कश्चित् सकृत् अश्नाति मासम् भवति तर्पितः || ४-३७-३०

If one eats for one time, a little of those divine and heart-pleasing fruits and tubers that have taken their origin from that oblational food material, he remains satiated for a month.

This is further corroborated by the reference to Hanuman's journey across the Himalayas to reach Kailasha. In the trans–Himalayan region, there are three notable jointed mountains: Kailasha, Rishabha, and Mahodhaya (also known as Oshadhi Mountain) (*Yuddhakanda* 74.31–33; 101.31–33). The southern slopes of Oshadhi Mountain were thickly forested, and these forests were rich in plants with curative properties, described in the epic as "glowing" and "aromatic." The entire region was permeated by a pleasant fragrance, emphasizing the importance of the area. Valmiki specifically highlights the significance of Oshadhi Peak as a sanctuary for medicinal plants, further elevating its spiritual and practical value.

In the epic, during the fierce battle between Ravana's forces and Rama's army, Lakshmana was grievously wounded and fell unconscious. As per the advice of the healer Sushena, Hanuman swiftly journeyed to the Dronagiri Hills and retrieved four powerful medicinal plants:

Mrita Sanjeevani (which has the power to restore life to the dead)

Vishalyakarani (which can extract weapons and heal wounds inflicted by them)

Suvarnakarani (which restores the body to its original complexion)

Sandhani (a potent herb capable of joining severed limbs or healing fractured bones) (*Yuddhakanda* 6.74.29–34).

These plants, drawn from the sacred peaks, played a crucial role in the healing and restoration of life, underlining the divine and medicinal importance of the mountains and their flora.

From Chitrakuta Hill regions

In addition to the Sanjeevani plant, the *Ramayan* mentions several other medicinal plants found in the regions surrounding Chitrakuta Hill, known for their healing properties. These plants are:

The Chitrakuta Forest is described in the *Ramayan* as a region rich in valuable medicinal plants, many of which were used for their healing properties by the characters in the epic. Some of the notable plants mentioned in the text include:

Svetakanthakari (*Solanum virginianum*) – A species of nightshade, often used in traditional medicine for its anti-inflammatory and analgesic properties.

Brahmi (*Bacopa monnieri*) – A revered herb in Ayurvedic medicine, known for its cognitive-enhancing effects and its ability to improve memory and mental clarity.

Katuka (*Picrorhiza kurrooa*) – A medicinal herb traditionally used to treat liver disorders and digestive issues, also valued for its immune-boosting properties.

Ativisha (*Aconitum heterophyllum*) – Known for its role in treating fever, digestive issues, and various infections, though it must be used with caution due to its toxicity.

Hilamocika (*Euhydra hincha*) – A lesser-known medicinal plant, which, like the others, was believed to possess healing qualities, though its specific uses are less documented in contemporary sources.

Heart-leaved moonseed (*Tinospora cordifolia*) – Known for its immune-boosting and anti-inflammatory properties.

Gymnema (*Gymnema sylvestre*) – Used for controlling blood sugar levels and as a treatment for diabetes.

Prickly chaff-flower (*Achyranthes aspera*) – Known for its use in treating respiratory ailments and inflammation.

Indian Squill (*Urginea indica*) – Used as a traditional remedy for heart and respiratory conditions.

Black Musali (*Curculigo orchioides*) – Often used to improve vitality and as an aphrodisiac.

Wild yam (*Dioscorea bulbifera*) – Known for its medicinal uses related to digestion and inflammation.

Ticktree (*Desmodium gangeticum*) – Used for treating kidney problems and as an anti-inflammatory.

Ivy guard (*Coccinia grandis*) – Used for its beneficial effects on blood sugar levels.

Cordia macleodii – Known for its use in treating wounds and other ailments.

Indian laurel (*Litsea glutinosa*) – Used for its aromatic and medicinal properties.

Indian Trumpet (*Oroxylum indicum*) – Used for its anti-inflammatory and digestive properties.

Trumpet flower (*Stereospermum suaveolens*) – Used for its medicinal value in treating skin diseases.

Indian kino tree (*Pterocarpus marsupium*) – Known for its ability to support digestive health and treat diabetes.

Arjun (*Terminalia arjuna*) – Widely known for its use in heart health and strengthening the cardiovascular system.

Belleric myrobalan (*Terminalia bellirica*) – Known for its detoxifying and digestive benefits.

Ink nut tree (*Terminalia chebula*) – Used for its purgative and digestive properties.

Peacock's tail (*Actiniopteris radiata*) – Used traditionally in treating various ailments.

Nut grass (*Cyperus rotundus*) – Known for its anti-inflammatory and analgesic effects.

Purple fleabane (*Vernonia cinerea*) – Used in traditional medicine for treating fever and inflammation.

Country Mallow (*Sidacordifolia*) – Used for its anti-inflammatory and analgesic properties.

Jungle grape vine (*Ampelocissus latifolia*) – Known for its use in treating digestive issues.

Panicled peristrophe (*Peristrophe paniculata*) – Used for its diuretic and anti-inflammatory effects.

Sickle senna (*Cassia tora*) – Used for its laxative properties and to treat skin conditions.

Lollipop climber (*Diplocyclos palmatus*) – Known for its use in treating various ailments.

Coat buttons (*Tridax procumbens*) – Used for its wound-healing properties.

Gulf leaf-flower (*Phyllanthus fraternus*) – Known for its ability to treat liver and kidney disorders.

Asian scalystem (*Elytraria acaulis*) – Used traditionally to treat a variety of health conditions.

Black nightshade (*Solanum nigrum*) – Known for its anti-inflammatory and analgesic effects.

Blue wiss (*Terminus labialis*) – Used for its medicinal benefits.

Five-leaf chaste tree (*Vitex negundo*) – Known for its use in treating joint pain and inflammation.

Indian mallow (*Abutilon indicum*) – Used for its anti-inflammatory and analgesic properties.

Broom creeper (*Cocculus hirsutus*) – Known for its use in treating a variety of ailments.

Indian Sarsaparilla (*Hemidesmus indicus*) – Used for its detoxifying and cooling effects.

Indian Gentian (*Enicostemma hyssopifolium*) – Known for its digestive properties.

Hogweed (*Boerhavia diffusa*) – Used to treat a variety of ailments, including liver and kidney disorders.

Yellow-berried nightshade (*Solanum virginianum*) – Known for its use in treating various health issues.

East Indian screw-tree (*Helicteres isora*) – Used for its medicinal properties.

Bengal quince (*Aegle marmelos*) – Known for its digestive and medicinal benefits.

Sage-leaved alangium (*Alangium salvifolium*) – Used for its medicinal value.

These plants were recognized for their therapeutic value and were integral to the healing practices described in the epic. Their presence in the *Ramayan* reflects not only the natural abundance of the forest but also the deep connection between the characters in the epic, the flora around them and wellness in ancient Indian traditions.

Other Economically Useful Plants

The *Ramayan* offers rich descriptions of the diverse vegetation and its uses, illustrating both practical and symbolic significance in ancient Indian life.

Punnaga (*Alexandrian laurel*), a valuable garden tree, known for its fragrant flowers, which yielded scented materials (*5.10.23*). Bamboo, a common forest tree, is mentioned as thriving along the banks of the Yamuna River (*2.55.8*) and was utilized for various purposes, including making rafts for crossing rivers (*2.55.14*) and constructing pillars and rafters for cottages (*3.1.21*). In fact, Lakshmana used bamboo to build the pillars for the straw cottage that he constructed for Rama and Sita (*3.15.21-23*).

Bilva (*Bengal quince*) trees were employed as sacrificial posts during rituals (*1.4.22*), and their fruit was also noted for being edible (*2.94.8*). Additionally, the wood of the bilva tree was one of the materials used in the construction of the bridge to Lanka (*6.22.55*). The poles of the Cutch tree were also used as yupas (ritual posts) during sacrifices (*1.4.2*).

The Indian mesquite, a large tree in the Panchavati forest (*3.15.18*), had its spreading branches used to build the roof of Rama's cottage at Panchavati (*3.15.22*). Bakula (*Indian medlar*) trees were used in constructing bridges (*6.22.59*), while the fragrant flowers of the Mango tree were added to food to make delicacies (*5.10.25*), and the wood was utilized in crafting weapons of war (*6.59.77*).

The Kovidara (*Mountain ebony*), also known as Raktapushpa (*Fire flame bush* or *blood-flower*), is particularly notable for being the emblem on Bharata's chariot flag. This flag, as Lakshmana recounts to Rama, symbolizes Bharata's arrival and the potential for it to come under their control in battle (*2.96.18-21*). These references to the various trees and their uses not only underscore their importance in daily life but also reflect their sacred and practical roles in the epic's narrative.

Fish and Sea life

Fish and Sea Life

There are only few references of Fish or sea food in *Ramayana*. First reference come along with the narration of 'Guha' the king of Nishadas. It is seen that Guha offer some fruits, meat, dried fish, and honey to offer to Bharat and his army.

इति उक्त्वा उपायनम् गृह्य मत्स्य मांस मधूनि च |
अभिचक्राम भरतम् निषाद अधिपतिर् गुहः || २-८४-१०

After uttering thus, Guha the king of Nishadas took fish, meat and honey as an offering and approached Bharata.

अस्ति मूलम् फलम् चैव निषादैः समुपाहृतम् |
आर्द्रम् च मांसम् शुष्कम् च वन्यम् च उच्च अवचम् महत् || २-८४-१७

"Here are the roots and fruits gathered by my tribe as well as fresh and dried meat of great quality and of various kinds, and all a produce of the forest."

Later in Kishkindha Kand, Kadambha praises the beauty of Pampa Lake and while explaining it he mentions that Rama and Laxman can find many birds, best fishes, red-crabs, and blunt-snouted small porpoises, and a sort of sprats, which are neither scraggy, nor with many fish-bones to eat.

निस्त्वक्पक्षानयसतप्तानकृशात्रैककण्टकान् - यद्वा -
निः त्वक् पक्षान् अयस तप्तान् अकृशान् न अनेक कण्टकान् || ३-७३-१५

तव भक्त्या समायुक्तो लक्ष्मणः संप्रदास्यति |
भृशम् तान् खादतो मत्स्यान् पंपायाः पुष्प संचये || ३-७३-१६

"Oh, Rama in that Pampa Lake there are best fishes, red-carps, and blunt-snouted small porpoises, and a sort of sprats, which are neither scraggy, nor with many fish-bones.

Lakshmana will reverentially offer them to you on skewering them with arrow, and on broiling them on iron rod of arrow after descaling and de-finning them."

In Yuddha Kand, when Rama prayed the Sea god to suggest the way to cross the ocean however the god the careless ocean did not appear in his personal form to Rama, even when it was requested to do so. Rama becomes angry at the ocean and loses fierce arrows, which cause a terror among the creatures inhabiting the sea. Here there is a mention of sea life such as oyster shells, fishes and crocodiles and sea elephants.

सशन्ख शुक्तिका जालम् समीन मकरम् शरैः || ६-२१-१९
अद्य युद्धेन महता समुद्रम् परिशोषये |

"I will make the ocean with its multitude of conches, oyster shells, fishes and crocodiles, dry up now in this great battle"

Rama, Sita, and Meat consumption

Rama, Sita, and Meat Consumption

I have explored the references to meat consumption in relation to Ravana, Kumbhakarna, and the broader context of the Rakshasas in other chapters in this book. Here, my focus is on presenting textual references from Valmiki's Ramayan that pertain to the Rama, Lakshmana, Sita, and Bharata.

Valmiki's Ramayan consists of 537 chapters and over 24,000 verses, structured into six Kandas, or books. While the text contains a few references to meat in relations with Rama, there are over a hundred mentions of a vegetarian diet. However, there is no direct reference to Rama, Lakshmana, or Sita consuming meat.

The first reference appears in the Ayodhya Kanda when Rama prepares to leave for his exile. As he approaches his mother, Kausalya, to deliver the heart-wrenching news, he finds her offering him a platter of nourishing food, lovingly prepared as a gesture of maternal care and affection.

चतुर्दश हि वर्षाणि वत्स्यामि विजने वने |
मधु मूल फलैः जीवन् हित्वा मुनिवद् आमिषम् || २-२०-२९

Rama said, "I shall dwell in the solitary forests for fourteen years, living as a sage, forsaking all luxuries, and subsisting on roots, fruits, and honey."

The term 'aamisham,' often misinterpreted as meat in some translations, has stirred debates among scholars. In its original context, it likely signifies food derived from natural, organic sources, excluding processed or indulgent items. Rama's declaration underscores his ascetic resolve and adherence to dharma, symbolizing simplicity, and renunciation. Aamisham meaning the covetousness or greed.

In Vedic tradition, when a son leaves home to study the Vedas and Shastras in a Gurukul, he reassures his parents that he will adhere to strict moral principles and remain steadfast in his religious duties. Consider a modern parallel: a student promising his parents before moving into a hostel, "I will not consume alcohol while I'm there." This does not imply that he drinks at home; rather, it is a reaffirmation of his commitment to discipline. In the same spirit, Shree Rama assures His mother that He would never compromise His values.

Notably, ancient Indian texts like the *Ramayan* and *Mahabharata* employ symbolic vocabulary, whose meanings often shift based on context. The misinterpretation of the term *aamisham* as "meat" likely stems from its evolving usage in later periods when it came to denote non–vegetarian food. Understanding this linguistic nuance not only clarifies the term's original intent but also underscores the complexity of translating ancient scriptures.

In Chapter 27, Sita persistently urges Rama to take her along into exile, expressing her unwavering commitment to adopting his way of life. She assures him that she will sustain herself on roots and fruits, just as he does. This clearly indicates that both Rama and Sita subsisted on a diet of fruits, roots, and honey during their time in the forest.

फल मूल अशना नित्यम् भविष्यामि न संशयः |
न ते दुःखम् करिष्यामि निवसन्ती सह त्वया || २-२७-१५

Sita said- "I shall live only on roots and fruits always, no doubt. Living along with you, I shall not create any unpleasantness to you."

Moreover, in almost all the verses of chapter 94, Shree Rama glorifies the various fruits, trees, and flowers at the forest of Chitrakuta, with absolutely no reference to any meat–eating whatsoever.

Later in chapter 52 of Ayodhya kand, there is a reference where Rama and Laxman hunted four deer and took the portions and reached to a tree where they rested for the night. There is no direct description on they are consuming the meat however they carry the portions along with them. The Sanskrit word used here is medhyam means "pure portion" although medhyam also translate to Barley.

तौ तत्र हत्वा चतुरः महा मृगान् |

वराहम् ऋश्यम् पृषतम् महा रुरुम् |

आदाय मेध्यम् त्वरितम् बुभुक्षितौ|

वासाय काले ययतुर वनः पतिम् || २-५२-१०२

Having hunted there four deer, namely Varaaha, Rishya, Prisata; and Mahaaruru (the four principal species of deer) and taking quickly the portions that were pure, being hungry as they were, Rama and Lakshmana reached a tree where they rested for the night.

Another such prominent reference comes at the time of Gruhapravesh (Housewarming ceremony) ritual Parna Kuti Laxman built for their stay Chitrakoot. Rama and Laxman performed the ritual where they use meat of Antelope. The same is also described in the topic of Meats in rituals in the book.

इणेयम् श्रपयस्वैतच्च्वालाम् यक्ष्यमहे वयम् |

त्वरसौम्य मुहूर्तोऽयम् ध्रुवश्च दिवसोऽप्ययम् || २-५६-२५

Rama said- "Oh, gentle brother! Boil this antelope's meat. We shall worship the leaf-hut. This day and this instant also are of a distinctive character. Be quick."

स लक्ष्मणः कृष्ण मृगम् हत्वा मेध्यम् पतापवान् |
अथ चिक्षेप सौमित्रिः समिद्धे जात वेदसि || २-५६-२६

Then, Lakshmana the strong man and son of Sumitra, killing a holy back antelope, tossed it in an ignited fire.

तम् तु पक्रम् समाज्ञाय निष्टप्तम् चित्र शोणितम् |
लक्ष्मणः पुरुष व्याघ्रम् अथ राघवम् अब्रवीत् || २-५६-२७

Feeling certain that it is cooked and heated thoroughly with no blood remaining, Lakshmana spoke to Rama the lion among man as follows:

अयम् कृष्णः समाप्त अनाः श्रृतः कृष्ण मृगो यथा |
देवता देव सम्काश यजस्व कुशलो हि असि || २-५६-२८

Laxman said- "This black antelope, with its complete limbs, has been cooked completely by me. Oh, Rama resembling God! Worship the concerned deity, as you are skilled in that act."

रामः स्नात्वा तु नियतः गुणवान् जप्य कोविदः |
सम्ग्रहेणाकरोत्सर्वान् मन्त्रन् सत्रावसानिकान् || २-५६-२९

Rama, the virtuous man and the learned man in chanting of sacred spells, after taking bath and with subdued mind, briefly chanted all the sacred scripts to be chanted at the end of a purifactory ceremony.

This entire description shows that Laxman knows the killing of animal and its processing. Rama used that animal for the housewarming /purification ceremony. There is no direct reference of consumption by Rama, Laxman, and Sita.

It is evident in the epic that the kings of Ikshvaku dynasty used to go for hunting as an exercise. As a Kshatriya it is common for them to go for hunting as preparation for battles and wars. One such reference is mentioned in chapter 63 of Ayodhya Kand where King Dasharatha recalling his earlier sin where he killed a young man by mistake. Later this story popularly known as Sharavan Bal story.

Here Dasharath uses the word 'vyaayaama krita samkalpah' meaning with a wish to do (Hunting as) an exercise.

तस्मिन् अतिसुखे काले धनुष्मान् इषुमान् रथी |
व्यायाम कृत सम्कल्पः सरयूम् अन्वगाम् नदीम् || २-६३-२१

*Dasharath said- "With a wish to do hunting as an exercise
in that most comfortable season, I went along Sarayu River,
in a chariot, wearing bow and arrows."*

Later in chapter 84, Guha the king of Nishadha seen to be instructing his people to make necessary arrangements to guard the river assuming that Bharat with his army is coming to kill Rama. He clearly instructs to take meat, roots, and fruits along with them to guard the river in their boats. Then he proceeds towards Bharat.

तिष्ठन्तु सर्व दाशाः च गन्गाम् अन्वाश्रिता नदीम् |
बल युक्ता नदी रक्षा मांस मूल फल अशनाः || २-८४-७

*"Let all our ferrymen guarding the river, along with
the troops, eating meat roots and fruits (in their boats),
stay positioned along the River Ganga."*

इति उक्त्वा उपायनम् गृह्य मत्स्य मांस मधूनि च |
अभिचक्राम भरतम् निषाद अधिपतिर् गुहः || २-८४-१०

*After uttering thus, Guha the king of Nishadas took fish, meat and
honey as an offering and approached Bharata.*

Guha offered some fruits and roots along with some fresh and dried meat to Bharat and his army.

अस्ति मूलम् फलम् चैव निषादैः समुपाहृतम् |
आर्द्रम् च मांसम् शुष्कम् च वन्यम् च उच्च अवचम् महत् || २-८४-१७

"Here are the roots and fruits gathered by my tribe as well as fresh and dried meat of great quality and of various kinds, and all a produce of the forest."

आशंसे स्वाशिता सेना वत्स्यति इमाम् विभावरीम् |
अर्चितः विविधैः कामैः श्वः ससैन्यो गमिष्यसि || २-८४-१८

"I hope the army, after eating well, can halt for the night here. Furnished with all you could desire, you can continue your journey tomorrow along with your troops."

Later in chapter 87, When Guha enquires Bharata about his intention towards Rama, Bharata clarifies him that he is proceeding to Rama's place to bring him back to Ayodhya. Bharata eases himself thereafter and asks Guha to report further details about Rama. Guha then started sharing the details and he informs that even though he offered various kinds of food to Rama, the latter refused it.

अन्नम् उच्च अवचम् भक्ष्याः फलानि विविधानि च |
रामाय अभ्यवहार अर्थम् बहु च उपहृतम् मया || २-८७-१५

"Various kinds of food and drink and different varieties of fruits were brought repeatedly by me to the presence of Rama for the purpose of his consumption."

तत् सर्वम् प्रत्यनुज्ञासीद् रामः सत्य पराक्रमः |
न हि तत् प्रत्यगृह्णात् स क्षत्र धर्मम् अनुस्मरन् || २-८७-१६

Rama, the truly courageous man, refused all of them. Reminding himself of his warrior's statute, he could not accept it.

Most of the confusion arises with below two verses in chapter 96 of Ayodhya Kand.

तां तथा दर्शयित्वा तु मैथिलीं गिरिनिम्नगाम् |
निषसाद गिरिप्रस्थे सीतां मांसेन चन्दयन् || २-९६-१

Having shown Mandakini River in that manner to Sita, the daughter of Mithila, Rama set on the hill-side in order to gratify her appetite with a piece of flesh.

इदं मेध्यमिदं स्वादु निष्टप्तमिदमग्निना |
एवमास्ते स धर्मात्मा सीतया सह राघवः || २-९६-२

Rama, whose mind was devoted to righteousness stayed there with Sita, saying; "This meat is fresh, this is savoury and roasted in the fire." (Fruit pulp and roasted kand mule)

"Mamsa" or "mansa" also has a meaning other than meat. "Mansa" also means the flesh of a fruit, or 'The fleshy part of a fruit.' In the South Indian temple town of Sri Rangam, when priests offer mango to Shree Ranganatha, they chant the prayer, iti amra mamsa khanda samarpayami: "I offer mango–mamsa (mango flesh) for the Shree to eat." Thus, even if there are occasional references to mamsa, we should know they refer to fruit pulp.

It can be again argued that Rama roasted it in fire, and we don't roast fruits. People can also say that "māmsa" here means roots and roots can be roasted.

Famous story of the Golden deer – Maareecha

There is a famous story of Mareecha (the demon capable of changing his body into various looks. Ravana asked him to come with him and be like golden deer to attract Sita. They came near the place where Rama, Sita and Laxman were staying. Sita indeed got attracted by the looks of that deer and she insists Rama and Laxman to capture the deer. In this entire episode Sita never mentioned to capture it for consumption. In fact, she keeps mentioning that if Rama could capture the deer alive, they can take it to Ayodhya after completion of exile period. It will be great attraction point to all including Bharat and her mother in laws. Even if the deer does not capture alive, she wishes to sit along with Rama on its golden deerskin, overlaying it on a seat of tender darbha grass-blades. They can use it like aasana (carpet like seat).

यदि ग्रहणम् अभ्येति जीवन् एव मृगः तव |
आश्चर्य भूतम् भवति विस्मयम् जनयिष्यति || ३-४३-१६

"It will be surprising if this deer draws into your capture alive and well, as it creates astonishment to one and all."

समाप्त वन वासानाम् राज्य स्थानाम् च नः पुनः |
अंतःपुरे विभूषार्थो मृग एष भविष्यति || ३-४३-१७

"When we return to kingdom on completing our dwelling in forest this deer becomes a masterpiece in palace-chambers for us."

भरतस्य आर्यपुत्रस्य श्वश्रूणाम् मम च प्रभो |
मृग रूपम् इदम् दिव्यम् विस्मयम् जनयिष्यति || ३-४३-१८

."Oh, Shree, the form of this deer creates an excellent jubilation to Bharata, to you the son of the nobleman, to my mothers-in-law, and also to me in palace-chambers."

जीवन् न यदि ते अभ्येति ग्रहणम् मृग सत्तमः |
अजिनम् नरशार्दूल रुचिरम् तु भविष्यति || ३-४३-१९

"Else if that best deer does not come into you capture while alive, oh tigerly-man, at the least its gorgeous deerskin will be remnant of it."

निहतस्य अस्य सत्त्वस्य जांबूनदमय त्वचि |
शष्प बृस्याम् विनीतायाम् इच्छामि अहम् उपासितुम् || ३-४३-२०

"I wish to sit along with you on its golden deerskin, overlaying it on a seat of tender darbha grass-blades, in case the deer is felled. [3-43-20]

As Sita insisted, Rama set out to capture the golden deer. Shortly after, Sita and Laxman heard Rama's voice calling for help. Concerned, Sita urged Laxman to go to his aid. With both Rama and Laxman away, Ravana seized the opportunity to approach Sita in the guise of a Brahmin ascetic. He was draped in a smooth, saffron-coloured robe, his hair neatly tied in a tuft. He wore wooden sandals, carried an umbrella on his right shoulder, and bore a staff on his left, from which a small water vessel was hooked. Welcoming the ascetic, Sita offered him hospitality, assuring him that her husband would soon return with forest produce and meat.

समाश्वस मुहूर्तम् तु शक्यम् वस्तुम् इह त्वया || ३-४७-२२
आगमिष्यति मे भर्ता वन्यम् आदाय पुष्कलम् |
रुरून् गोधान् वराहान् च हत्वा आदाय अमिषान् बहु || ३-४७-२३

***"Be comfortable for a moment, here it is possible for you
to make a sojourn, and soon my husband will be coming
on taking plentiful forest produce, and on killing stags,
mongooses, wild boars he fetches meat, aplenty.***

There are two key observations to be made here. First, there
is no mention of the famous 'Laxman Rekha'—the protective line
supposedly drawn by Laxman around the hut to safeguard Sita. This
detail may originate from sources other than Valmiki's Ramayan.

Another intriguing aspect is that Sita appears to offer meat
to the ascetic. Given that he is disguised as a Brahmin, this raises
a significant question—how could she offer meat to someone who,
according to common understanding, follows a dietary restriction
against its consumption? The next verse provides some clarification
on this matter. Sita is addressing him as 'oh, Brahman...' and yet
asking his caste.

सः त्वम् नाम च गोत्रम् च कुलम् आचक्ष्व तत्त्वतः |
एकः च दण्डकारण्ये किम् अर्थम् चरसि द्विज || ३-४७-२४

***"Such as you are, oh, Brahman, you may make mention
of your name, parentage and caste, in their actuality.
For what reason you are wandering in Dandaka forest lonesomely?"
Thus Sita questioned Ravana.***

Sri K. M. K. Murthy explains this quite effectively. "This is a
tricky stanza. This implies her knowledge and/or ignorance about
Ravana. Sita is from a well-trained family, she is not supposed to
question the caste, creed, and name of a real sanyaasi. Again, she is

asking him to reveal himself 'in essence, truthfully.' She might have thought him to be a cursing Brahman in the first instance, but she might have found him out to be a pseudo-sanyaasi. Now that she is slowly realising that he may not be a proper Brahman either, she may be asking him straightforwardly. Because Ravana is coming out of Brahman's guise in next two stanzas, it is said that she pointedly asked him as above."

Later, Rama strikes the golden deer with his arrow, revealing its true form as the demon Mareecha. As Mareecha falls, his illusionary deer body vanishes, exposing his original demonic form. At this moment, Rama realizes that he has been lured into a trap. Despite this, he hunts another deer and takes it to Sita, demonstrating his unwavering commitment to fulfilling his promise. Having assured Sita that, he would bring her the deer, Rama chooses to honour his word rather than return empty-handed.

निहत्य पृषतम् च अन्यम् मांसम् आदाय राघवः |
त्वरमाणो जनस्थानम् ससार अभिमुखः तदा || ३-४४-२७

Raghava then on killing another spotted deer and on taking its flesh, he hurried himself towards Janasthaana.

Jatayu, the great bird, meets Rama and Lakshmana and recounts his battle with Ravana, revealing that Ravana abducted Sita and fled southward. Determined to find her, Rama and Laxman continue their search in that direction, eventually encountering the demon, Kabandha. A fierce battle ensues, and Rama slays Kabandha. Before his death, Kabandha pleads with Rama to incinerate his body so that he may regain his divine form. He admits that his current hideous state is a result of his past arrogance, expressing repentance for his actions. Initially, both Rama and Kabandha are wary of each other, leading to a cautious exchange of words. However, upon being cremated, Kabandha is restored to his celestial form and offers crucial guidance to Rama. He advises Rama to seek out Sugreeva, who, like Rama, is in dire need of support to overcome his troubles. Kabandha urges Rama to befriend Sugreeva, as their alliance would be mutually beneficial. He provides directions to Mount Rishyamuk, where Sugreeva resides, encouraging Rama to forge an alliance with him in his quest to rescue Sita.

Kabandha praises the beauty of Pampa Lake and while explaining it he mentions that Rama and Laxman can find many birds, best fishes, red-carps, and blunt-snouted small porpoises, and a sort of sprats, which are neither scraggy, nor with many fishbones to eat. As per my understanding these words by Kabandha are from his point of view. Although there are no direct mention of Rama and Laxman consuming any of this later during their stay near the Pampa Lake area. They spend entire rainy season (almost 4 months) there before they marched towards Lanka with Vanar sena.

न उद्विजन्ते नरान् दृष्ट्वा वधस्य अकोविदाः शुभाः || ३-७३-१३
घृत पिण्ड उपमान् स्थूलान् तान् द्विजान् भक्षयिष्यथः |

"Thereabout birds will be unflustered on seeing humans, because they are artless to avoid hunting, because none kills them, and you may savour them because those birds will be best and burley, similar to ghee-gobs.

रोहितान् वक्र तुण्डान् च नल मीनान् च राघव || ३-७३-१४
पंपायाम् इषुभिः मत्स्यान् तत्र राम वरान् हतान् |
निस्त्वक्पक्षानयसतप्तानकृशात्रैककण्टकान् - यद्वा -
निः त्वक् पक्षान् अयस तप्तान् अकृशान् न अनेक कण्टकान् || ३-७३-१५
तव भक्त्या समायुक्तो लक्ष्मणः संप्रदास्यति |
भृशम् तान् खादतो मत्स्यान् पंपायाः पुष्प संचये || ३-७३-१६

"Oh, Rama in that Pampa Lake there are best fishes, red-carps, and blunt-snouted small porpoises, and a sort of sprats, which are neither scraggy, nor with many fish-bones. Lakshmana will reverentially offer them to you on skewering them with arrow, and on broiling them on iron rod of arrow after descaling and de-finning them."

Further when Hanuman visits Lanka in search of Sita, He finds Sita in Ashoka Vatika. When they start conversation Sita, filled with longing and concern, inquiries about Rama, Hanuman reassures her by describing his disciplined way of life in the forest. He tells her, "Rama neither consumes meat nor indulges in intoxicating drinks. Every evening, he sustains himself with the simple food found in the forest, carefully gathered, and arranged for him. His thoughts are always with you, Sita, and he endures every challenge with the hope of being reunited with you soon."

न मांसं राघवो भुङ्क्ते न चापि मधुसेवते ।

वन्यं सुविहितं नित्यं भक्तमश्राति पञ्चमम् ॥ ५-३६-४१

"Rama is not eating meat, nor indulging even in spirituous liquor. Everyday, in the evening, he is eating the food existing in the forest, well arranged for him."

Dr. R Rangan says "Cause of Rama's rejection of meat and alcohol need not be taken as Sita's separation as few do. The statement (well-prescribed) here proves Rama follows the prescription. Some ask if Rama never drinks when Hanuman particularly mentions Rama's non–consumption of liquor? Generally, Kshatriyas consume liquor. Seeing Rama's pious life where he avoids meat and alcohol, Hanuman admires it as a great virtue."

Dr. R Rangan conclude that there are ample number of references in the epic which clearly says Rama does not consume meat in forest–life and very few evidence of meat consumption can be rejected as interpolation. To reconcile, we must see that his meat eating is extremely rate or highly occasional in his forest life.

Sri K.M.K. Murthy provides a great overview about Vegetarianism of Rama as a foot note in chapter 73 of Aranya Kand.

It is important to remember that Rama was a Kshatriya. Even during his exile, he did not fully adopt the ascetic lifestyle of a muni (sage). He remained with his wife, carried weapons like a warrior, and actively protected sages and hermits by slaying many demons.

In the Treta Yuga, Kshatriyas were permitted to consume the meat of five specific five-nailed animals—porcupine, wild boar, monitor lizard, hare, and turtle—as part of the Ayurvedic dietary system. However, when it comes to the Supreme Rama, the key question remains: did he consume meat or not?

We find that Rama made a solemn vow to his mother, Kausalya, that he would abstain from meat during his exile. Given his unwavering commitment to dharma, it is certain that he upheld his word, regardless of circumstances.

This raises another important question—if Rama abstained from meat, why were he and Lakshmana engaged in hunting various animals in the forest? The answer lies in the multiple purposes of hunting during their time in exile:

As food for guests, including Rishis and other visitors–Hospitality was a key aspect of dharma, and providing appropriate food for sages and guests was customary.

As raw material for weaponry and essential tools – Animal products were often used in crafting bows, strings, and other equipment.

As materials for practical use – Animal skins were commonly used as mats for sitting, especially for meditation or meals.

Thus, while Rama adhered to his vow of abstinence from meat, hunting served other necessary and dharmic purposes during his time in the forest.

Additions Beyond the Valmiki Ramayan

Ramayana is so popular in India that every region has their own association and own folk storis, art with Rama. Most of these are not mentioned in Valmiki Ramayan, rather later additions. I am trying to list few famous examples of such additions. One such famous story of Shabari is already discussed in this book in a separate chapter.

Rama Phal, Sita Phal, Laxman Hanuman Phal *(phal- Fruits)* are incredibly famous in India. These were names after the main characters in *Ramayana* much later.

Rama Phal- After the famous war with Ravan and killing Ravan in the war. Shree Rama visited Rishikesh to perform penance, to get rid of the dosha of killing a Brahmin. At this time, during penance, he subsisted on these fruits which were later named after him. This is called prickly pear which is extensively used in European countries as well. The Mexican government uses this symbol in official documents.

Sita Phal- Sita phal is named after Sita the Goddess of Ramayan. Sitaphal is our very own custard apple that is known to have its roots in South America. Some say it reached through Portugal in the 17th century. The legend associated with this fruit goes thus. When Ravan abducted Goddess Sita and rushed to Lanka in Pushpak Vimaan, the highly distressed Sita shed copious tears, every drop of which, along with her sweat, moistened the earth but instead of getting absorbed in the soil, they a very special variety of plant started growing, with each glistening tear from her eyes, a plant grew up in response. These plants, when they grew, fruits that tasted a lot different from the ordinary fruits. When the fruits were broken open by vanaras much later, they saw that these fruits were full of seeds covered by white pulp looking like tear drops. The tears of Goddess showed up as fruits that were named after Sita.

Lakshman Phal– Lakshman Phal or soursop is grown in Brazil. It is believed to be a miracle food for cancer patients which clinically is supposed to have helped many patients with TB, Cancer, AIDS and so on.

Hanuman Phal– Hanuman phal, or soursop, belongs to the custard apple family. It is green coloured and prickly to touch with an edible white pulp and it is full of seeds. It is used to make confectionaries and is being seriously experimented in Cancer research.

Rama Kand Mool (Rama Kand)

The Ramayan mentions that Shree Rama subsisted on simple foods, such as kand mool, also known as 'Rama kand mool' or simply Rama kand. This tuber, shaped like an elephant's foot, is typically served in thin slices, eaten raw, and often seasoned with lime, salt, chili powder, honey, or jaggery. Believed to be the flowering stalk of the century plant (Agave Sisalana), Rama kand has a cool and mildly sweet taste. Rich in starch, it helps quench thirst, provides nourishment, and has a cooling effect on the body.

Rama kand grows in hilly, forested regions near water sources and is found across India. In Karnataka, it is referred to as Bhoochakra gadda (Maerua Oblongifolia). Its availability aligns with Shree Rama's journey through the forests, particularly in the Aaranya Kaand section of the Ramayan.

Although I searched for specific references regarding this Valmiki's text, but could not find direct mentions. However, there are general references to foods like phal-mool (fruits and tubers), which could encompass such items.

Amaranth (Rajgira)

Another food associated with Shree Rama is amaranth (*Amaranthus hypochondriacus*), commonly known as *chaulai* or kingseed. It is referred to as *Ramadana* in North India, meaning 'the seed gifted by Shree Rama,' and as *rajgira* or 'royal grain' in Central India, symbolizing the divine gift from the royal figure of Shree Rama. This versatile seed can be consumed in a variety of forms, including *Ramadana roti*, *chaulai ka saag*, *chaulai ka raita*, *Ramadana kheer*, *Ramadana halwa*, *Ramadana laddu*, and *Ramadana chikki*.

Although *Ramadana* is not classified as a grain, but rather as a non-cereal, it is consumed as part of a *phalahaar* (fruit-based) diet during fasts. Popped amaranth grain soaked in milk is a popular dish for breaking fasts, particularly during religious festivals. Additionally, popped amaranth seeds are used to prepare *Ramadana laddus*, considered pure and fit for offering to the gods.

The root of the amaranth plant, known as *ratanjot* or cockscomb, holds significant value as well. It imparts a vibrant red hue to dishes like the Kashmiri delicacy *rogan josh*, showcasing its culinary and cultural importance.

Ragi and Rice Competition

A popular folk tale from Karnataka narrates a debate between rice and ragi over their superiority. When Shree Rama asked Hanuman to choose, he deferred, suggesting a test. Sage Gautama gathered the grains, and rice, revered in rituals, claimed superiority, dismissing ragi as inferior. To settle the dispute, Shree Rama ordered both grains to be stored for six months. When presented in Ayodhya, rice had spoiled, while ragi remained fresh. Ragi declared the winner, praising its resilience and nutritional value, emphasizing its role in sustaining farmers and communities.

Conclusion

According to the research of Nilesh Oka Sir, the Ramayan era dates back approximately 14,000 years(12209 BC). It is fascinating to observe that many of the foods consumed during that time continue to be an integral part of present-day Indian cuisine. The food culture of the Ramayan period was remarkably rich and advanced, reflecting a deep understanding of culinary traditions and nutrition.

The kingdom of Ayodhya was prosperous, flourishing with an abundance of cereals (dhana dhanya), livestock such as horses, camels, cows, and donkeys. The economy was primarily agrarian, with cattle playing a crucial role. Various cereal crops, including paddy, wheat, barley, sesame, and lentils, were widely cultivated.

Vedic rituals prominently featured numerous food substances, such as milk, yogurt (dahi), clarified butter (ghee), and honey—staples that continue to be essential in Indian households today. Additionally, there was extensive knowledge of medicinal plants, and the use of medicinal oils was well established, reflecting an advanced understanding of health and wellness.

The food culture of the time was remarkably rich, as people possessed knowledge of a wide variety of dishes and palatable side dishes. Rice-based desserts, dumplings made from cooked pulses, and an array of dairy products—including curds, butter, ghee, and cheese—are mentioned in historical texts. Feasts were lavish, often featuring silver dishes filled with sugar candy, showcasing the culinary sophistication of the era.

The diet of the Vanar Sena in the Ramayan reflected their life as forest dwellers, primarily consisting of fruits, roots, and honey.

Their sustenance was deeply connected to the natural abundance of the forests, highlighting a harmonious relationship with their environment.

The consumption of meat and wine was common in certain societies and often featured in grand feasts. The Rakshasas are frequently depicted as predominantly carnivorous, consuming distinct types of meat, including human flesh. Many of them, especially those residing in deep forests and remote regions, were portrayed as fearsome man-eaters. Meat consumption was an established practice in specific communities, reflecting the diverse dietary habits of the time

The consumption of wine (madira) and other alcoholic beverages was prevalent, particularly in contexts associated with royal luxury, celebrations, and occasional indulgence. References to wine often highlight its role as a symbol of pleasure, hospitality, and decadence—much like in the present day.

The society of the time was remarkably advanced, as evident from descriptions of the grand capitals of Ayodhya and Lanka. The architectural marvels, including seven-story buildings and magnificent palaces, reflect an advanced civilization. The use of metals such as gold, silver, and iron further highlight their technological progress. Additionally, references to the Pushpak Vimana and various advanced weapons suggest a sophisticated understanding of engineering and warfare.

॥ श्री सीतारामचन्द्रार्पणमस्तु : ॥

Annexture

Table 1 – Eatable plants in Ramayana

S.No	Sanskrit Name	Common Name	Botanical Name	Reference in Ramayana
1	Abhisutah	Soma, Mooon Plant	*Sarcostemma brevistigma*	1.14.6
2	Agnimukh/ Bhallatak	Indian marking nut tree (Bibba)	*Semecarpus anacardium*	3.72.52 2.56.7
3	Aja	Bishop's weed (Ajwain)	*trachyspermum*	2.91.67
4	Amlaki	Indian Gooseberry Amla	*Phyllanthus officinalis*	2.91.51
5	Atimuktaka	Phobi Nut tree (Bibba)	*Hiptage benghalensis*	3.75.24
6	Badari	Indian Jujube	*Zizyphus mauritiana*	
7	Bhallataka	Cashew nut	*Anacardium occidentale*	2.56.7
8	Bhavya	Dillenia (KaRamabel) Elephant apple	*Dillenia indica*	2.94.8
9	Bijpur	Citron Buddha's Hand Mahalungi or Mitha limbu.	*Citrus medica*	2.91.30

S.No	Sanskrit Name	Common Name	Botanical Name	Reference in Ramayana
10	Biva	Bengal quince (Bel)	*Aegle marmelos*	1.4.22 1.24.15 2.56.71 2.94.8 3.11.74 3.60.13 6.22.57
11	Bimb	Little gourd/ Ivy gourd (Marathi-Tondle)	*Coccinia grandi*	5.15.29
12	Chanak	Bengal Gram Chick Pea Harbhara/ Chana	*Cicer arietinum*	7.91.20
13	Chuta	Mango	*Mangifera indica*	2.91.30 3.3 4.1.80 5.10.25 5.14.3 6.4.72 6.59.77 7.42.2

S.No	Sanskrit Name	Common Name	Botanical Name	Reference in Ramayana
14	Dadima	Pomegranate	*Punica granatum4*	3.60.21 6.22.59 7.42.5
15	Dhanwan	Phalsa (Phalsi)	*Grewia asiatica*	2.94.0
16	Godhuma	Wheat	*Triticum aestivum*	3.16.16
17	Hintal	Mngrove Date Palm	*Phoenix paludosa*	4.27.18
18	Ingudi	Desert date (Hinganbet)	*Balenites aegyptiaca*	2.50.28
19	Ikshu	Sugar Cane	*DhaRamabo, JhRamabi, or Ota.*	
20	Jambu	Jambolan Black plum Java–plum Jamun/ Jambhul	*Syzygium cumini*	2.55.15 2.91.51 3.71.3 14.28.19 4.20.30 7.42.5
21	Kadali	Banana	*Musa paradisiaca*	2.20.3 2.117.80 3.36.13 3.42.22 3.62.4 3.42.13

S.No	Sanskrit Name	Common Name	Botanical Name	Reference in Ramayana
22	Kaleyak	Saffron Autumn crocus	*Crocus sativus*	
23	Kalpa vrik-sha	Indian kapok/ Silk cotton tree	*Salmalia malabarica*	4.34.5
24	Kapith	Elephant -apple Wood apple	*Limonia acid-issima*	2.91.20
25	Karir	Caper plant	*Capparis deciduas*	6.22.59
26	Karpur	Camphot tree Japanese camphor	*Cinnamomum camphora*	4.28.8
27	kASH	Fodder cane Wild sugar cane	*Saccharum spontaneum*	2.88.22
28	Khadira	Black catechu Betel-nut (Supari)	*Senagalia catechu*	1.4.2 3.15.18
29	Kharjura	Date sugar plam Wild date palm	*Phoenix sylvestris*	3.15.16 4.2.9
30	Kimsuka	Bastard-teak Bengal kino (Palas)	*Butea monosperma*	2.63.9 2,63.8,9 4.1.82 5.15.8 5.54.34 6.40.14

S.No	Sanskrit Name	Common Name	Botanical Name	Reference in Ramayana
31	Kovidara	Mountain -ebony (Kanchan)	*Bauhinia*	2.84.3
32	Kritmal	Golden shower Purging cassia Bahava	*Cassia fistula*	4.27.18
33	Kulitha	Horse Gram kulthi, hulaga, or kuleeth.	*Dolichos biflorus*	7.91.20
34	Lakuch	Monkey Jack wotomba	*Artocarpus lakoocha*	3.15.18
35	Lodhra	Asiatic sweetleaf	*Symplocos crataegoides*	4.43.13
36	Madhuka	Indian butter tree Moha	*Madhuca longifolia*	2.94.9 3.11.74 3.15.21 3.42.17 6.4.79
37	Maskar	Bleck Pepper	*Piper nigrum*	3.15.21
38	Mugda	Black Grama Urad	*Vigna mungo*	7.91.19
39	Narikel	Coconut	*Cocos nucifera*	3.35.13 4.42.11
40	Neevar	Asian rice	*Oryza sativa*	2.61.5

S.No	Sanskrit Name	Common Name	Botanical Name	Reference in Ramayana
41	Padmak	Sour cherry Himalayan wild cherry	*Prunus cerasoides*	2.76.16
42	Panasa	Jack fruit	*Artocarpus integrifolia*	2.91.30 2.94.8 3.15.16 3.60.21 3.73.3 6.31.29
43	Parnas	Holi basil (Tulasi)	*Ocimum tenuiflorum*	3.15.18
44	Pippali	Indian long pepper	*Piper lonh=gum*	3.11.29
45	Priyal	Charoli	*Buchanania lanzan*	2.94.8
46	Sarshap	Celery cabbage	*Brassica campestris*	2.25.28
47	Shar	Tall cane	*Saccharum bengalense*	3.15.22
48	Slesh maataka	Indian cherry (Ladosa)	*Cordia myxa*	1.14.22–23

S.No	Sanskrit Name	Common Name	Botanical Name	Reference in Ramayana
49	Tala	Palmyra-palm toddy palm	*Borassus flabellifer*	2.91.50 3.35.13 3.44.16 3.60.18 4.40.53 5.18.11 5.56.36 6.22.56 6.39.3 6.67.159 6.77.61
50	Tamala	Sour mangosteen	*Pimentra racemosa*	2.91.50
51	Tamala	West Indian Bay tree DhaRamabo, JhRamabi, or Ota.	*Garcinia xanthochymus*	2.91.50 3.15.16 3.35.23 4.27.17 4.42.11 6.39.3
52	Tila	Asian Rice	*Oryza sativa*	2.69.10
53	Tilaka	Sesame	*Sesamum orientale*	2.91.50

S.No	Sanskrit Name	Common Name	Botanical Name	Reference in Ramayana
54	Timisha	Ash gourd White Pumkin	*Benincasa hispida*	2.94.8 3.15.15 3.15.18 4.1.92
55	Uddalaka	Coconut palm	*Cocos nucifera*	4.1.81
56	Udumbara	Cluster Fig	*Ficus racemosa*	2.14.34 2.55.14
57	Vanir	Rattan caen palm	*Calmus rotang*	4.27.18
58	Vistar	Bread flower	*Vallsris solanacea*	2.20.28

References

1. https://www.valmikiRamayan.net/utf8/vr_index.htm

2. PLANT AND ANIMAL DIVERSITY IN VALMIKI'S RAMAYAN and Animal diversity in Valmiki *Ramayana*- M. Amirthalingam. C.P.R. Environmental Education Centre, Chennai. 2013.

3. PLANTS OF RAMAYAN NBRI. Res. PUBL No. 311 (NS) K. M. Balapure, J. K. Maheshwari & R. K. Tandon *National Botanical Research Institute, Lucknow – 226 001, India.*

4. Wines in ancient India- D K Bose 1922

5. Literary evidence of agricultural development in ancient India, Lagnajeeta Chakraborty. International Journal of Sanskrit Research 2021; 7(2): 32-35

6. Medicinal Plants of *Ramayana* period, International Journal for Exchange of Knowledge; 2 (1): 41-44, 2015 Dipti Varma.

7. Ramayan Insights-I, Dr. R. Rangan, WEBOLIM, India.2023

8. https://sanskritdictionary.com

9. https://www.wisdomlib.org/definition/mamsa

10. All images AI generated.

9 798897 249800